THE SCARED CHILD

THE SCARED CHILD

Helping Kids Overcome Traumatic Events

Barbara Brooks, Ph.D.
and
Paula M. Siegel

John Wiley & Sons, Inc.

New York • Chichester • Brisbane • Toronto • Singapore

The text is printed on acid-free paper.

Copyright © 1996 by Barbara Brooks, Ph.D., and Paula M. Siegel
Published by John Wiley & Sons, Inc.

All rights reserved. Published simultaneously in Canada.

The information contained in this book is not intended to serve as a replacement for professional medical advice or professional psychological counseling. Any use of the information in this book is at the reader's discretion. The publisher and the authors specifically disclaim any and all liability arising directly or indirectly from the use or application of any information contained in this book. The appropriate professional should be consulted regarding your specific condition.

Library of Congress Cataloging-in-Publication Data:

Brooks, Barbara.
    The scared child : Helping kids overcome traumatic events / Barbara Brooks and Paula M. Siegel.
        p.   cm.
    Includes bibliographical references.
    ISBN 0-471-08284-8 (pbk. : alk. paper)
    1. Post-traumatic stress disorder in children—Prevention.
2. Psychological debriefing.   3. Parent and child.   I. Siegel, Paula M.   II. Title.
RJ506.P55B76   1996
155.9'3—dc20   96-10330

Printed in the United States of America

10 9 8 7 6 5

To Jennifer Brooke Silverman
BB

To Melissa F. Coren
PMS

CONTENTS

PART TWO

WORKING THROUGH TRAUMATIC EVENTS

PREFACE

As is the case for many people, my professional interest in children and traumatic events began as a result of a personal experience. In 1980, a colleague's son's fourth-grade teacher died unexpectedly. The child and his classmates were shocked and frightened. Working with the school, my colleague and I developed a school-based intervention designed to help the children deal with this tragic event. Afterward, we were able to see that talking about what they saw, felt, and thought made the children less distressed and better able to function at school, in their families, and with friends. This lesson stayed with me and was the first step in shaping my thinking about children and trauma.

It is an unfortunate reality of life that terrible things happen. One need only listen to the news on a regular basis to know that despite all of your desires, you cannot shield your child from life's occurrences. Hurricanes happen. School classmates commit suicide or are killed in automobile accidents. Pets die. I have found that what comes naturally to parents (and adults in general) is to try to protect their children from such experiences by ignoring or avoiding discussion of them, believing that their children will not understand or that they will forget in time. I have learned, however, that these experiences have effects on children even if the child does not fully understand or cannot fully recall the event. The real job is to help children develop the coping skills necessary to overcome the effects of traumatic events. Rather than trying to "make it better" through denial, we can help our children through these traumatic experiences by providing opportunities for them to talk and by learning to listen to them. This book details a four-step method for listening to and communicating with your child when a crisis has occurred.

Since 1983, I have been Director of Clinical Services for an off-site employee assistance program (EAP). Our clients are employees of specific companies who have retained our firm's services. Employees consult with EAP counselors for many kinds of family and personal problems. Parents bring their children to the program when they are having difficulty with normal transitions, such as getting ready for school, or as a result of extraordinary events, such as a frightening hospital experience or a natural disaster like Hurricane Andrew. The lessons I had learned from the intervention with the fourth-graders led me to develop a method of working with children individually that was as helpful to the child as the group intervention had been.

In addition to counseling individual employees and their families, our EAP also provides consultation to corporate managers and human resource personnel. When hurricanes, earthquakes, bombings, or homicides affect the workplace and the employees, our professional counselors respond. We are mental-health disaster workers. My colleagues, Wini Atkinson and Paula Stern, and I have traveled around the country to respond to these modern-day catastrophes. Our job is to set up programs to help employees and their families in the aftermath of a tragedy. We are onsite quickly and set up "debriefing" teams. We meet with employees individually and in groups, and we meet with children in groups.

Through repeated exposure, my colleagues and I have refined the debriefing technique I first used with the fourth-graders. We have trained fifty social workers, psychologists, and psychiatrists from the largest mental health agency in the United States to use this debriefing method in the event of community disaster.

In this book, I attempt to take the reader through the process of helping children understand and cope. I offer age-appropriate strategies and suggestions and, based on my experience, explain what to say, what to do (and not do), and how to listen to your child when something terrible happens in your life or in the life of a child. I hope that you find this book useful in helping you help your child or in recognizing when professional help may be required.

In several parts of this book, I discuss case examples. These examples are based on aggregates and composites and do not represent real individuals. I wish to emphasize that the case examples do not show children or parents suffering from mental illness. Rather, their responses are normal, expected reactions to abnormal events, with the children struggling to maintain equilibrium in the face of overwhelming tension and anxiety and the parents expressing appropriate concerns of parents whose children had been thrust, by circumstance, into a crisis experience.

I have structured the book to appeal not only to parents, but to a wider audience as well. In fact, this book is meant as a tool for all adults who are in a position to touch, in a meaningful way, the lives of children. Pediatricians, teachers, school guidance counselors, grandparents, aunts, uncles, and family friends, as well as parents, are often called on in a crisis and will benefit from reading this book. It is also addressed to my colleagues in the mental health profession who may find it a useful guide for themselves and a tool for the parents who consult them.

BARBARA BROOKS, PH.D.

ACKNOWLEDGMENTS

I want to acknowledge my "debriefing colleagues" and compatriots, Paula Stern and Wini Atkinson, for their support and wisdom, and for their laughter and culinary habits. They can always be counted on to do their best, and their best is very good indeed. To the others who gave generously of their time and advice—my son Rick Silverman, for his meticulous layperson's parsing through of the various drafts of this book; his wife, Jeanne Codron, for her encouragement and patience; my son Gary Silverman, and his wife, Marion Silverman, for their comments and insights as young parents—I say thanks.

Sunnie Singer, C.S.W., read through several of the chapters and gave her trained opinion, for which I am grateful. Many other professionals have contributed to this book through my understanding of their published research and writing. If there are mistakes, they are mine alone.

To the kids who survived hurricanes, earthquakes, homicides, divorce, or abuse, and who shared their story with me, I am eternally indebted. Your humor and courage keep me going. I wish the grownups of the world could promise you a lifetime free of violence and full of caring. You deserve it.

On behalf of myself and my coauthor, Paula Siegel, I would also like to thank Janet Manus, our agent, for bringing us together and making this book possible, and PJ Dempsey, our editor, without whose patient guidance and attention this book never would have come to fruition.

HOW TO USE THIS BOOK

This book contains three parts. In the first part, you'll get an overview of trauma and its various forms and effects. Chapters 1 to 3 introduce you to the concept of trauma and its effects on people. You'll learn about how the effects of trauma are different in children and adults. Some of the different causes of trauma are explored, and you'll learn how to recognize the effects of trauma—psychological, emotional, and physical—in children of different ages. In Chapter 4, I explain debriefing, the four-step method that I use to help a child cope with a trauma that he or she has experienced.

Examples of how the four-step debriefing works are given in the second part in Chapters 5 to 10 on death, abuse, natural disasters, divorce, illness and injury, and trauma by proxy (when a child is traumatized by something that happens to someone else). I caution that although Chapters 5 to 10 apply debriefings, they do not repeat all of the pertinent information about debriefing contained in Chapter 4. If you are looking for information about a specific type of trauma, you must read the discussion of the specific trauma in conjunction with Chapter 4.

In the third and final part, you'll find the resources you might need to help a child through a trauma. At several points in the book, I mention that professional help might be useful. Indeed, this book is intended to provide only general guidance, as each case is unique. In all cases, if the symptoms seem especially acute or if you fail to notice a decrease in symptoms after debriefing, you should promptly seek the advice of a mental health professional. In Appendixes 1 and 2, you'll find information on finding a therapist and what to expect from therapy. Appendix 3 contains a reading list of books recommended for adults and/or children concerning trauma in general and specific events, such as illness, divorce, and natural disaster, in case you want to read further on the topic.

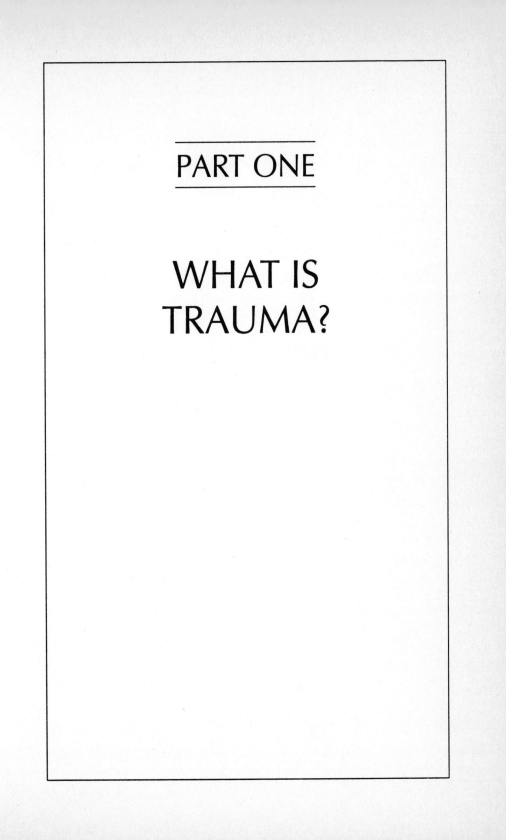

PART ONE

WHAT IS TRAUMA?

1

TRAUMA

An Overview

U nlike the minor crises that are part of the normal travails of life, traumas are situations that are outside the range of expected experience.

- Being evacuated for a hurricane is annoying. Being at home when a hurricane blows and rains is a normal crisis in the tropics. Having a hurricane take away your home and your whole neighborhood is traumatic.
- Having a parent die of old age is sad but expected. Having a parent die suddenly when you are still a child is traumatic.
- Seeing a person being robbed is shocking. Seeing someone shot during a robbery is traumatic.

Traumas often overwhelm the coping skills we all use to handle the expected problems in life, and they strip us of our sense of security. This book focuses on children's responses to traumatic events and what we as adults can do to help them.

THE TYPES AND CAUSES OF TRAUMA

Following is an overview of the traumatic situations I address in this book and the reasons they cause trauma.

Death

For adults, the trauma caused by the death of a loved one is sometimes mitigated when the loss is an expected one, occurring after a
long illness or in advanced age. For children, however, there is no
such thing as an expected loss. Children believe that their world is
stable, that the people who are in it today will be in it tomorrow and
forever. Thus any death is a shock. Even the death of a pet can have
a traumatic effect on a child.

The death of a parent is particularly traumatic for young children
because parents play so many roles in normal childhood development. For example, children use the parent of the same sex as a role
model to form their self-identity. Children use the parent of the opposite sex to understand their sexual identity, so the loss of that parent
affects development as well.

If a death is the result of unnatural causes, such as an act of
violence, a suicide, or an accident, it is a trauma for all concerned.
Adults sometimes hold themselves responsible for such tragedies.
"If only I had been there, I could have protected him." "If only I had
taken a different route, the accident wouldn't have happened." Children also feel that sense of responsibility. They blame themselves for
situations for which they in no way could be responsible.

In addition, children are angry after an unnatural death. They are
angry that the person is gone, that he or she was taken from them.
Angry feelings are more common when a death is violent or accidental than when it is the result of natural causes.

Sexual Abuse

Sexual abuse is traumatic because it violates a child's basic sense of
trust, particularly if the child is being abused by a parent. If you can't
trust your parents, whom can you trust?

Sexual abuse also blurs normal family boundaries. Mothers and
fathers are supposed to sleep together and have sex with each other.
Children are not supposed to have sex with parents or other adult
relatives.

Another way that sexual abuse causes trauma is by providing a
premature introduction to sexuality. Such abuse is overstimulating
and leads to an age-inappropriate interest in sexual matters. Young

children are not supposed to be sexually active, and they don't have a normal means for discharging the sexual tension that can build as a result of sexual abuse. To discharge some of the tension, young children may begin to masturbate a lot and talk incessantly about sexual matters.

Sexual abuse interrupts a child's normal development. School-age children who are sexually abused have difficulty concentrating in school, which is a primary task for those years. Abused children also feel different; they feel like they're freaks. Their sense of belonging to the group is taken away from them. When a school-age girl is having sex with her father, how can she feel like other girls her age who are giggling about boys and talking about kissing someone someday?

Physical Abuse

Physical abuse is obviously traumatic because of the pain that it causes, but more pointedly because the painful violence is inflicted by someone who is supposed to love and care for the victim. Children often cope with and rationalize physical abuse by beginning to believe that they are at fault and deserve the beating. If their parents (who are supposed to love them) hit them, they believe they must be bad.

One of the consequences of the ongoing trauma of physical abuse is the use of violence by the child to get what he or she wants. Violence begets violence, and the child's use of violence just creates more problems in the outside world for the abused child.

Natural Disasters

Natural disasters are traumatic because of the general disruption they cause to the whole community. There's no place where life feels familiar. There's no place where the victims can feel safe and comfortable. For children, school and family life are disrupted. Even if the parents don't lose their jobs, often the regular caregiver can't find a way to get to the house, or the parents can't find a way to get the children to the caregiver's home.

Youngsters are traumatized by some natural disasters because of their suddenness. Without warning, a violent act of nature can separate children from their families. Children feel vulnerable and worry that such a separation could happen again and that perhaps the next time they won't be able to find their families.

Though natural disasters are traumatic, there are aspects of them that mitigate the trauma. Unlike other traumas, natural disasters don't single out one individual, and they are not a result of one person harming another. Because the whole community shares the devastation, it comes together as a support network.

Divorce

The most traumatic aspect of divorce is the conflict that wells up between the parents, which can continue for years. Second is the loss of the family unit. In the majority of cases, divorce means the loss of the noncustodial parent—most often the father. Children grow up with the idea that they can trust their parents' relationship to each other and their own relationship to their parents. Divorce breaks apart those notions. Children whose parents divorce feel that relationships can't be trusted. That's a theme that haunts them through young adulthood and makes attachments to others difficult.

Illness and Injury

Illness and injury are traumatic because they are usually unexpected. Life is going along normally and suddenly something terrible happens—the diagnosis of cancer or a serious car accident. The illness or injury may happen to the child or to someone close to the child. Because the terrible event happened during a normal part of life, children can become uncomfortable with ordinary things. If a car hits a child on a bicycle, she may no longer feel comfortable riding her bike or even riding in a car. Or, if a child's mother is suffering from cancer, the child may fear that every physical ache and pain means that he, too, has cancer.

Illness and injury also bring the child into the health-care system either as a patient or a visitor. Most adults are not particularly fond of hospitals. For a child, it is truly scary. For the youngster, terrible things happen in hospitals. As a patient, the child is stuck with needles, given shots, hooked up to intravenous lines, and given medication that sometimes has serious side effects, such as hair loss. As a visitor, the child sees all of these terrible things happening to a loved one, and that is frightening. The child sees the healthy parent distraught over the illness of the spouse. Mom puts on a brave face when she goes into the room to visit Dad, but she wipes tears from her eyes and blows her nose all the way home in the car. Family life is also disrupted as the healthy spouse reorganizes the household schedule to accommodate the hospital's visiting hours. Maybe Mom isn't home after school anymore. Instead, she's asked an aunt to baby-sit while she tends to Dad in the hospital.

Financial concerns also may play a role in this trauma if the major breadwinner is ill or injured and can't earn a living for some time. Even when there is disability insurance, it usually doesn't completely match the disabled person's customary income, and the family has to change its spending habits until the ill person gets back to work.

Trauma by Proxy

This is a trauma that a child feels as a result of an event that happened to someone else, which the child hears about, sees, or learns about through another person or, more frequently, the media. Most often, trauma by proxy occurs as a result of highly publicized events, such as the Oklahoma City bombing, the drowning murder of Susan Smith's two children, or the suicide of teen idol Kurt Cobain. These events are traumatic because children identify with the victims. The closer in age children are to the victims, the more traumatized they will be by the event. They think, even if they are not fully aware of it, "That could have been me in the car. Would my mother ever do such a thing?" or "I could have been in the day-care center in Oklahoma City when the bomb went off."

Trauma by proxy often involves events that are consequences of violence, random or otherwise. Children have a sense of powerlessness and feel that the world is a place where things are out of control. Whether the event takes place in Bosnia or Oklahoma City, the pictures of injured or dead children tell the same story: The world isn't safe. Not only isn't it safe, but the adults who would protect children are powerless against the forces that would hurt them.

This message is delivered in a very powerful way. Kids often learn about these horrible events from television or from graphic photographs on the covers of magazines and newspapers. These images are communicated in a very immediate way through the occipital lobes in the brain, so their effect is very powerful compared to something heard on the radio.

Such images in the news make people sit up and take notice of tragedies around the world. Adults think, "Oh, my God, we have to do something," and they begin relief efforts. Children have the same feelings of urgency and despair when they see images of devastation, but they don't know that the terrible event is happening on a different continent or that the situation is a horrible, once-in-a-lifetime event, rather than something that could happen again at any time. Preschoolers have no time or geographic frame of reference to understand that it is highly unlikely that they will be in a similar situation. They don't have the sophistication to channel their sense of urgency toward a relief effort. Instead, they are left with feelings of helplessness, fear, and insecurity, which are the aftermath of trauma by proxy.

Though this book focuses on these specific traumas, the coping skills that are offered to shepherd children through these traumas can be applied to other situations.

2

THE EFFECTS OF TRAUMA

Trauma overwhelms both children and adults and causes a number of physical and psychological reactions. Let's look at what happens to a person at the moment of the trauma and in the immediate aftermath of the event.

At the moment of crisis, all people of all ages react with a primitive survival response called the fight-or-flight response. It goes like this: Initially, there's a rush of adrenaline throughout the body that prepares us to make rapid movement. Then blood is directed to the brain. Our thinking is clearer, our vision is sharper, and our bodies are primed to move with speed and strength.

When the crisis is over, many people are unable to turn off the response. They remain jumpy and guarded in any situation remotely similar to the moment of terror. They may have trouble sleeping or concentrating. They are on edge most of the time and easily erupt in anger. Others, to avoid the feelings associated with the crisis, withdraw and cut off communication with those around them. To block out feelings and memories of the terrible event, they become numb and detached. They find that they are unable to connect with family members and friends the way they did before the incident.

The constellation of feelings and reactions that follows terrifying events is called posttraumatic acute-stress reaction. For adults and for children, posttraumatic acute-stress reaction is a normal response to an abnormal situation. As a consequence of the experience, many people are no longer able to use their normal coping skills to adapt to stressful situations. For many others, the posttraumatic acute-stress reaction will dissipate over time. In all cases, the debriefing method described in this book may assist with or speed the recovery from posttraumatic stress.

The ability to handle a traumatic situation without being over-whelmed depends on a person's coping skills, life experience, per-ception of the event, and emotional stability. For example, we are not surprised that a police officer is less stressed by observing a murder victim than most other adults would be. We know that prior exposure and training have "inoculated" the officer.

CHILDREN AND
POSTTRAUMATIC STRESS

Youngsters and teenagers find it difficult to make sense out of trau-matic events. They do not have the mature coping skills of an adult or the life experience that helps grown-ups put a trauma in perspec-tive and know that they will return to a normal life after the trauma. Moreover, children need their parents for protection, and in most traumatic situations parents cannot provide that protection. Parents can't stop a tornado from ripping off the roof of a house or flood-waters from washing away the child's toys. In illness or death, the crisis can involve a parent. In some traumatic situations, such as di-vorce or abuse, the parents are actually the cause of the crisis.

Because kids have inadequate coping skills and limited life ex-perience and feel the loss of parental protection, traumatic events cause feelings of helplessness and vulnerability. Children's sense of security is undermined by trauma. The feeling of safety is gone.

In the aftermath of a trauma, teenagers tend to act like trauma-tized adults, but younger children often don't. Youngsters may show baffling behavior in response to a trauma. We have all been struck by incongruous images of children having tea parties or playing catch in front of the twisted ruins of their homes after a tornado. Many of us have also been mortified by the silly antics of our children at a solemn funeral service or wake. What strikes us is how unaware children seem to be in the midst of a tragedy. While we openly wrestle with our fears and despair after a trauma, it appears as if the whole event went right over our children's heads. Why should we talk to them about it? It will only make matters worse. Right?

Wrong.

THE IMPACT OF TRAUMA ON KIDS

Research has shown that children of all ages do feel the fear and anxiety that follow in the wake of a trauma. Sometimes, however, their behaviors don't show it. Children can't stand feeling sad for long periods of time, so they turn their attention away from the trauma to their other world of imagination. However, their feelings of sadness and fear can come out in their play and in uncharacteristic behavior such as clinging, moodiness, or daredevil play (see Chapter 3).

Children don't grasp the nature of traumas in the same way adults do. Adults understand that natural disasters, grave illness, and even senseless violence are rare punctuations in the course of ordinary life. They may grieve for a sudden or expected loss, but they also look forward to reconstructing their lives. A child—particularly a young child—has no such perspective. Children don't understand what has happened, why it happened, and, perhaps most important, the unlikelihood of it happening again.

Because children have a limited perspective on life due to their age and because they are still developing their sense of self, they often internalize the anxiety and fear that a trauma causes. This internalized anxiety and fear can have a broad effect on their behavior after the trauma. Children who survive a car accident become fearful not only of being in a car, but of being near cars on the road or even traveling in buses. Suddenly, the school bus is menacing after such a trauma. Children who survive a natural disaster are fearful not only of another storm or earthquake, but also of being separated from their parents. Youngsters who had long ago mastered daily separation from their parents suddenly balk at leaving home to go to school or to a day-care center, and they cry when their parents leave for work. The trauma has left them with a sense that the people they love and depend on could be swept away at any moment. No longer can they count on their parents to pick them up every day.

Because the anxiety and fear following a trauma can take root in a developing child's psyche, it's particularly important to give children the support they need to put a trauma in perspective and move beyond it to develop normally. Parents can do much to help their children—whether they are toddlers or teens—cope with or even avoid the effects of a traumatic experience. We'll talk about how to do that in Chapter 4 and in Part 2 of this book.

POSTTRAUMATIC STRESS DISORDER (PTSD)

Some experiences are so extreme that they overwhelm both adults and children long after the trauma is over. When the intense symptoms of the posttraumatic acute-stress reaction persist for more than a month, they are no longer a normal response to trauma. Instead, they turn into what is known as posttraumatic stress disorder (PTSD), a psychological disorder in which the acute reaction to a trauma lingers long after the event itself is over.

What We Know about Posttraumatic Stress Disorder

Today we know that there are predictable patterns of emotional reactions following a trauma, but our early clues to the existence of PTSD were discovered in a very narrow segment of the adult population: soldiers. During World War I, when a soldier on the front lines developed overwhelming shame, guilt, fear, or nightmares, or isolated himself in a way that interfered with his performance in combat, he was diagnosed with shell shock and sent home. The theory was that the symptoms would resolve themselves once the soldier was taken off active duty. This didn't turn out to be the case, however, and most shell-shocked soldiers continued to be haunted by their war experiences (by flashbacks or otherwise) long after they were safely stateside.

Recognizing their earlier failure, mental health professionals developed a new strategy for helping soldiers during World War II and the Korean War. Battle-fatigued soldiers were taken away from the front lines for individual psychiatric counseling and then sent back into battle. The idea behind this treatment was much like the cowboy ethic of getting right back on the horse after you fall off so that your fears don't have a chance to get the best of you.

Soldiers who couldn't "get back on the horse," whose symptoms stayed the same or worsened over time, were diagnosed as having an adjustment reaction. This meant that they had preexisting psychological problems that made it difficult for them to adjust to life on the front lines. In other words, it was believed that the traumatic experience of war wasn't the cause of the symptoms: the soldier's prewar psychological makeup caused the problem. We know now that this is not true.

The Vietnam War radically changed our ideas. Following the war, mental health professionals recognized that the core experience of war itself, rather than any preexisting psychological problem, was powerful enough to cause immediate and long-term psychological difficulties. A new name was given to the lingering constellation of symptoms experienced by many Vietnam veterans: posttraumatic stress disorder.

In an effort to help Vietnam veterans come to terms with their experiences, military psychologists and psychiatrists brought them together in groups to explore and share their feelings and fears. They found that such debriefings were more successful in diffusing posttraumatic stress than any of the approaches used previously.

Once it was recognized that a traumatic event could itself cause a psychological disorder, mental health experts turned their attention from the military population to the civilian population. They wondered whether they could take what they had learned from traumatized veterans and apply it to ordinary people who had been in extraordinary circumstances. In fact, when they interviewed people in the aftermath of natural disasters like earthquakes or terrible acts of violence such as torture or witnessing a murder, the researchers found that trauma survivors were more like soldiers in battle than unlike them. Following extraordinary events, ordinary people often develop the same pattern of symptoms of posttraumatic stress disorder as soldiers. The "battlefield" they were afraid to face was whatever had traumatized them: the earthquake, the torture, the murder.

Mental health experts also found that civilian trauma survivors responded to group intervention in ways similar to soldiers. These group sessions laid the groundwork for the development of the treatment we use with trauma victims today to prevent or abate posttraumatic stress disorder.

Symptoms of Posttraumatic Stress Disorder*

When people experience or witness an event that involves actual or threatened death or serious injury to themselves or others, they respond with intense fear, helplessness, or horror. For children, those feelings may be expressed by disorganized or agitated behavior. If the reactions categorized below last more than a month, they become signs of posttraumatic stress disorder.

- *Avoidance:* sense of numbing, detachment, or absence of emotional responsiveness; reduction in awareness of surroundings (e.g., being in a daze); feeling of not being oneself or watching from the outside; feeling of detachment or estrangement from others; inability to recall an important aspect of the trauma.
- *Reexperiencing:* persistently reexperiencing events in at least one of the following ways: recurrent images, thoughts, dreams, flashbacks, or distress on exposure to reminders of the traumatic event. In young children, repetitive play may occur in which themes or aspects of the trauma are expressed, or they may have frightening dreams without recognizable content from the trauma.
- *Increased anxiety:* difficulty sleeping, irritability, poor concentration, anger, hypervigilance, or restlessness.

*Source: American Psychiatric Association, *Diagnostic and Statistical Manual of Mental Disorders*, 4th ed. (Washington, D.C.: American Psychiatric Association, 1994).

3

RECOGNIZING SIGNS OF POSTTRAUMATIC STRESS IN CHILDREN

Before you can begin to help a child come to terms with a trauma, you must be able to look at the event through a child's eyes. How does a child perceive and cope with life-altering events?

HOW TO RECOGNIZE POSTTRAUMATIC STRESS IN CHILDREN

Very few generalizations can be made about how children respond to a traumatic event, because their perceptions differ dramatically by age. A four-year-old's experience of an earthquake is very different from a sixteen-year-old's. Consequently, the signs of posttraumatic stress will vary with the age of the child. In addition, just as adults differ in their response to and ability to cope with a crisis, children also have individual responses to trauma and unique coping capabilities. Even children close in age within the same family may respond differently to a traumatic event. Perhaps one child is more philosophical and another more emotional.

After working with many children of all ages who have survived traumas, I have recognized certain hallmark behaviors of posttraumatic stress that characterize different age groups.

15

Infants and Toddlers (Birth to Age One)

Infants and toddlers have difficulty communicating what happened
to them during a trauma. Thus, measuring the degree of impact (if
any) of such an event and treating it can be difficult. Very young
children who have been through a traumatic experience may exhibit
the following signs of distress:

*   They may fuss more.
*   They may "lose" developmental steps already acquired.
*   They may fail to learn new and expected developmental tasks.

Because infants and toddlers are not able to tell us how they feel,
dealing with trauma in children of this age is beyond the scope of this
book. Although I cannot address specific coping skills, very young
children need extra soothing, nurturing, and time with their parents
or other trusted caregivers after a traumatic event.

Preschoolers (Ages Two to Five)

The preschooler's outlook on life combines reality and magical thinking, resulting in a perspective that often has very little to do with
what really happened. For example, preschoolers may attribute
magical qualities to traumatic reminders. Thus, a child may say that
the monkey bars are bad or didn't like Annie or that the jungle gyms
might hurt him. Because preschoolers' understanding of the world is
limited, they are able to grasp only bits and pieces of information
about a traumatic situation. They then fill in the gaps with their
imagination. For instance, the preschoolers of South Dade County,
Florida, heard a lot about Hurricane Andrew as it drew nearer to their
community in August 1992. What they heard on television and radio
reports was that Andrew was huge. He was fast. He was dangerous.
And he had one eye. In their minds, Andrew was not a tropical storm
but a terrible monster with one eye who was drawing closer and closer
and would ultimately take away their homes and toys.

Children in this age group see events that have happened sequen-
tially as having a cause-and-effect relationship even when none actually exists. For instance, if a preschooler does something to make

her father angry and her dad has a car accident later that day, she is likely to think that she caused the car accident by being bad. Preschoolers believe, too, that their wishes and thoughts can make things happen. A young child who wishes, for instance, that his new sister would go away might very well feel that he is responsible if his sister becomes ill or dies.

Youngsters in this age group have a very self-centered outlook on the world and often feel that they cause many events over which they in fact have no influence. For instance, when their parents get divorced, kids in this age group often feel that they caused the breakup.

Young children often don't tell their parents about their feelings. They don't have the words to express what is going on inside of them, and sometimes they're afraid to let their parents know because they think they were the cause of the terrible event that befell the family. However, children in this age group communicate their posttraumatic stress in other ways.

For preschoolers, whose vocabularies leave them limited ways to verbalize their feelings of distress, the following behaviors can serve as a signal to parents.

Signs of Posttraumatic Stress in Preschoolers

- They may become anxious and clingy, not wanting to separate from their parents at nursery school or the baby-sitter's house.
- They may seem to take a step backward in development, sucking their thumbs, wetting their beds, refusing to go to sleep, or waking at night when they'd passed those stages long ago.
- They may become aggressive in their play with other children, with their parents, or with their own toys.
- They may play the same game over and over, like piling up blocks and knocking them down, dropping toys behind radiators or furniture and retrieving them, or crashing the same two cars over and over again.
- They may express magical ideas about the event ("The storm came because I was so mad" or "Daddy left because I was bad").
- Though they say they are having fun in an activity, they may look sullen, angry, or intense in a way that, to an adult, doesn't look much like they're having fun.

School-Age Children (Ages Six to Twelve)

School-age children have a greater awareness of the world around them than preschoolers, and they are much more able to grasp the nature of a traumatic event. There are benefits and drawbacks to this maturity. At this age, kids aren't plagued by the magical thinking that burdens preschoolers with the responsibility of everything that happens around them. They know that they don't cause another person's illness or death. They know that their wishes or thoughts do not bring about natural disasters. However, the more realistic outlook of school-age children makes them aware of the real threats of their world, and that can be very frightening. It's scary to find out that Mom and Dad cannot protect them against all dangers and that sometimes Mom and Dad are just as frightened and vulnerable as they are.

School-age children might keep to themselves after a traumatic event not because they don't know how to express their feelings, but because they don't want to burden their obviously distressed parents further. When school-age children put up a brave front, parents who are themselves overwhelmed by the trauma they've been through often want to believe that, for whatever reason, their children are sailing through the crisis unscathed. It's important, though, not to ignore behavioral signs of distress even when the child tells you that she's doing fine.

Signs of Posttraumatic Stress in School-Age Children

- They may revert to developmentally earlier coping mechanisms, such as an ego-centered view (i.e., thinking that someone died because they had bad thoughts about the person).
- They may compensate for feeling helpless during the crisis by blaming themselves for elements of what happened. Thinking that they caused the event gives children a sense of power and control. Helplessness painfully reminds them of being young and totally dependent.
- Their lack of control over the trauma may make them feel that their future is unsure, which can lead some children to act recklessly.
- They may experience a significant change in school performance. It's not uncommon for a child to have difficulty concentrating and performing in school after a traumatic event. On the other

hand, they may become intensely focused on schoolwork to the exclusion of having fun.

- They may test the rules about bedtime, homework, or chores. School-age children believe in rules. When a bad thing happens even though they obeyed the rules, children may become oppositional and testy.
- They may have an interruption in relating to a best friend.
- They may experience sleep disturbances. The child might have nightmares or difficulty falling asleep.
- They may join in reckless play. Where the preschool child will crash her trucks a hundred times, the school-age child might physically engage in dangerous games as a way of exhibiting a sense of control that was lost during the trauma.
- They may talk about the supernatural. Magical thinking still exists in this age group, though it takes a different form. Rather than believing in monsters, school-age children may show a fear of ghosts or other supernatural visions. A school-age child might say, for instance, that the ghost of his dead father came back to give the child the message that the father was okay.

Teenagers (Ages Thirteen to Eighteen)

Adolescents, or "almost adults," are an inherently erratic bunch, and their responses to trauma reflect their nature. They have a grown-up grasp of the reality of the traumatic situation, but their reactions can swing wildly from that of a mature adult to that of a young child. One minute they're asking what they can do to help out, and the next minute they're acting recklessly.

In a time of crisis, we often want to rely on the budding maturity of our teenage kids, and we can be impatient with their juvenile antics. It's important to keep in mind that their behavior is a sign of their vulnerability and a reminder that they still need reassurance from the adults around them.

Teenagers do not freely communicate with adults. What parent has not had the following conversation with a teen?

"Where are you going?"

"Out."

"What are you doing?"

"Nothing."

"How are you doing?"

"Fine."

It is especially important, therefore, to watch out for the telltale signs of posttraumatic stress in teenagers.

Signs of Posttraumatic Stress in Teenagers

- They often feel that only their peers can understand what they are going through, and they go to their peers for support. However, a marked shift in the relationship with the parents is cause for concern.
- They may get involved in risky behaviors, such as experimenting with drugs, becoming sexually active, or being truant from school, as a way of handling their anxiety and countering feelings of helplessness. Teens behave this way because after a trauma they often feel that their future is limited. They feel that whatever they're building toward could be wiped out in a minute, so planning for the future is pointless.
- They may develop a negative self-image because they were not able to avoid or alter the situation.
- They are likely to engage in revenge fantasies against the person or people they hold responsible for the trauma and then feel guilty about their vengeful feelings.
- They may experience a shift (either an intensification or withdrawal) in the normal developmental tasks of their age, such as dating, friendships, or sense of autonomy. A marked withdrawal from friends is a cause for concern. Teenagers may isolate themselves and show signs of depression. There is an increased risk of suicide.

Any sustained significant change in any child's typical behavior warrants attention. If you observe any pattern of the above signs but are not aware of any trauma having occurred to the child, set time aside to talk to him or her. If the behavior persists or becomes more acute, consult a professional.

Being able to recognize posttraumatic acute stress is the first important task in shepherding a child through the trauma. The next chapter discusses helping a child recover from a traumatic experience in an effort to prevent posttraumatic stress disorder.

4

DEBRIEFING

A Four-Step Method for Helping a Child through a Traumatic Experience

Debriefing offers a structure for listening and talking to the traumatized child. It tells you what to say so that the youngster will talk to you. Debriefing will help you find out how the child feels, and it will help the child understand what happened. It will make the child feel stronger and less vulnerable.

Debriefing is not counseling. It is a way for an involved adult to offer a forum for the child's expression of emotions and reactions. The goal is to normalize responses and aid recovery.

WHAT DEBRIEFING DOES

Debriefing

- Assists the child in "venting"
- Helps the child develop a more complete understanding of what happened
- Normalizes the child's responses
- Teaches the child appropriate coping skills
- Assists the child in adjusting to posttrauma life

Debriefing will not heal all of the emotional wounds of a trauma overnight, but it can put a child on a path of healing and resolution and can speed recovery from trauma.

Keep in mind that debriefings will likely have to be repeated for children. Very young children can't remember complicated things, and they need to hear the explanations of what happened over and over again and in different ways. For all children, subsequent life events bring back aspects of the original trauma. If a child's older brother was murdered while in his senior year of high school, you can expect that when the traumatized child reaches his senior year, he will experience anxiety. He will not simply project the past experience onto the current situation, but he will relive it to some degree. He will reconnect to the fears and anxiety that he felt at the time of his brother's murder, and he will go through the mourning process again, but with a greater understanding of what happened years ago.

So, too, when a parent dies, the surviving child relives the parental loss at milestone events, such as her graduation, on the occasion of her marriage, at the birth of her own children, when she becomes her deceased parent's age, and when her child becomes the age she was when her parent died.

Traumatic events are life-changing events. Children reexperience them many times for years after they are over. Each time the child reexperiences the trauma, the child may benefit from a debriefing.

HOW DEBRIEFING WORKS

Debriefing has four steps:

1. Preparing yourself
2. Having the child tell the story
3. Sharing the child's reactions
4. Survival and recovery

Though the process works best when completed within a single time period (from a few minutes to an hour), the steps can be done separately. Although I have given a time frame for the various steps, these are general estimates, not absolute limits.

You shouldn't rush to get through the steps as quickly as possible or cut the child off when you've reached the upper time limit suggested for a given step. Be sensitive to the child's readiness to go from one step to the next, and allow as much time as needed to explore the feelings in one step before moving on. It is important, however, to follow these steps in the order indicated to get results.

Step I: Preparing Yourself

For this step, take as long as you need. However, if you find that you are prolonging your preparation indefinitely and can't bring yourself to begin the next step with the child, you might not be emotionally ready to do the debriefing. You may be too distraught yourself or simply uncomfortable with doing the debriefing. In this case, consider finding a close friend or other family member to do the debriefing for you.

To make a debriefing as beneficial as possible, you can prepare in the following ways.

• *If more than one child was involved in the trauma, it is generally a good idea to debrief all of the children at the same time in a group.*   Group debriefing works well because the children learn from each other that they're not the only ones who feel scared or different or alone.

When younger kids hear older kids talking about how frightened they were, the little ones don't feel like big babies for being scared themselves. Children can also learn that acute stress reactions have a beginning, a middle, and an end. One child might say, "Right after the tornado, I had to have the light on at night to fall asleep. But now I'm not as scared anymore, and I can sleep in the dark again." A child who is still troubled by sleeping in the dark will realize that she won't feel as frightened forever. Listening to other kids tell their stories and talk about how they feel makes a child feel less alone, less like she's the only one who is having problems.

If there are no other children who can share the experience, that's okay because you can effectively use the debriefing with a single child.

• *Choose the best time to debrief.*   Timing is important. Debriefing should quickly follow the conclusion of the events. Debriefing for natural disasters, however, is more complicated because the conclusion of the traumatic event does not come when the storm or earthquake is over. The aftermath of the disaster prolongs the trauma.

When a child's home, neighborhood, and school are destroyed and you are absorbed in getting life back to normal, it is not a good time to debrief. Everyone is still living by the rules for survival: Be strong; don't think about it. Adults and children are not ready to discuss the disaster because it is not really over. You are not able to vent your feelings because you need to keep going and to maintain a single focus. This is also true for the children. When things settle down and everyone breathes a sigh of relief, that is the time to debrief. In my experience, this occurs between two and five weeks after a natural disaster.

- *Choose an appropriate time of day and an appropriate place.* Afternoons when most kids are hungry, tired, and cranky are not a good choice. Children are often most approachable in the early part of the day, but you know your child's inner clock best. If your child is more likely to get into sharing his thoughts just before bed, a good time to choose is the quiet time right after dinner.

  The debriefing doesn't have to be done at home. If your child has a favorite thinking spot, you might want to have your private time there. Teenagers, for instance, like to talk as they walk or toss a ball or sit in a coffee shop or diner.

- *Keep it private.*   Ask someone else to answer the phone and the door. Make sure that others in the house know that you don't want to be interrupted.

- *Find out what really happened.*   Be a detective, and get as many details beforehand as possible from sources other than your child. Children sometimes leave out significant parts of an experience because they're too scary to think about or because they blame themselves for what happened. This is the information you're looking for to counter fears and correct misperceptions. The more you know before starting the debriefing with your child, the better you'll be able to help your child.

- *Prepare yourself to hear things you might not have expected.* You'll need to brace yourself and remain calm if you hear unexpected and perhaps unpleasant things. For example, in an abuse situation, you may not have realized the full scope of what occurred. If you overreact when your child talks to you, he or she will clam up. One of the most important parts of a debriefing is to get the child to talk about his or her experience.

- *Educate yourself about posttraumatic stress and be prepared to reassure the child.* Review Chapters 2 and 3 on posttraumatic stress reactions. Although posttraumatic stress is normal, it can provoke worrisome behavior. Children who haven't wet the bed in years may do so several nights in a row. Some who had mastered sleeping alone now cry for you to keep them company while they fall asleep. Others may show survivor guilt or become depressed.

  It's important for children to know that these and other expressions of anxiety are perfectly normal, *temporary* reactions. If you are familiar with the symptoms of posttraumatic stress, you will be in the best position to give reassurance. Think of chicken pox. *You* know that the itchy rash is a nasty but temporary scourge, and you can assuage the fears of a child who expects to be covered with this weeping, itching rash forever. If you weren't familiar with the symptoms of chicken pox, you wouldn't be able to say, "It'll go away soon," when your child gets upset. Chances are, you'd be just as disturbed by the sight of the rapidly spreading sores, and you'd make the child even more anxious.

  That's what happens after a trauma if you don't know the common behaviors that children exhibit. Instead of soothing anxieties, you can exacerbate them by needlessly getting upset over a child's reverting to thumb-sucking or bed-wetting or feeling guilty, and that can prolong the posttraumatic stress reactions. Armed with the basic facts about posttraumatic stress, you can defuse the fears of children of any age and help them feel secure.

- *Be realistic when reassuring.* Adults often think that the best thing to do is to tell the child that everything will be all right even when they know that problems lie ahead. Such blanket reassurances do not help the child because they give him a false sense of security. A better approach is to let the child know that you will be there to love and protect him even if everything isn't all right.

- *Understand that crying or the need to be comforted is not a sign of weakness.* It's natural to accept crying and fussing in little ones after a trauma, but you may be less accepting of older children who cry and want comforting. You might feel that the right approach is to admonish them to get it together and not make such a big deal over what happened. On the contrary, children of all ages need comfort and reassurance after a trauma. Even teenagers who are normally brash and independent may be unnerved and suddenly clingy. Giving children the attention they need is the best way to help them "get it together" in this situation.

- *Hear their fear.* Don't say that you know what the child is feeling. You don't, and saying this cuts off rather than encourages conversation. Adults often think that this statement shows their sympathy, but instead kids often interpret it to mean that you don't want to hear what they have to say. Asking a child what happened and how she feels shows your concern and willingness to listen.

- *Don't be too eager to correct misunderstandings.* If the child's story doesn't jibe exactly with what you know happened, you may be inclined to correct the child's impressions on the spot. Don't. It's better to wait until the child has had a chance to express all feelings and experiences. Breaking into the story too early to point out misinterpretations makes kids feel that you're not willing to accept their experience or that you are criticizing or belittling them. You will not discover what they saw and felt.

- *Be willing to say nothing.* Sometimes the best thing you can do is just listen quietly. Adults are eager to offer comfort and allay fears. Sometimes they are simply impatient with the length of time a child can take to tell a story. However, it's important for youngsters to know that you're interested in what they have to say and are willing to hear them out. Be sure to give your child time to gather his or her thoughts.

- *Never blame the child.* Do your best to listen nonjudgmentally, and never blame the child for what he is feeling—even if the child expresses anger, resentment, or pleasure. These feelings are normal in the face of a traumatic event.

- *Don't make a schedule by which you think your child should recover.* Each child recovers from a trauma in his or her own time. Even in the same family, brothers and sisters grapple with their reactions to a trauma in different ways and in different time frames. If you see a gradual acceptance of the event, you know that the child is on the right track. Be concerned if the child seems to get worse or seems unable to come to terms with a traumatic situation. If this happens, it's an indication that you might need the help of a mental health professional who works with children and who is familiar with posttraumatic stress (see Appendixes 1 and 2).

- *Don't assume that boys handle things better than girls.* Our society still harbors some traditional notions about how boys and girls react in a crisis. Put these assumptions aside, and remember that all children—boys and girls—are upset by a trauma. All kids—no matter what their age or gender—should be allowed to cry and be comforted.

These points may seem like an awful lot to remember, but they can make the difference between reaching out successfully to help children and alienating them or driving them into silence, which can only prolong and deepen the aftereffects of trauma. So take your time with them, and get them fully in your grasp before going on to step II of the debriefing.

Step II: Having the Child Tell the Story
(Five to Twenty Minutes)

Letting children tell the story helps them express their feelings about what happened and piece together important facts. Let your child describe the incident in his or her own way. You want to discover what the child experienced during the event. The adult's job is to assist the child in describing his or her experience of the traumatic incident, whether the child was victim, witness, or perpetrator.

Here are four techniques to help your child tell the story. You can use them separately, but they are even more effective when used in combination, especially with younger kids who may have trouble expressing themselves with words.

- *Telling a story by talking:* This is the most straightforward method for debriefing a child. Help the child along with questions when necessary by using your background knowledge of the event. If a class was held hostage by a gunman and the child didn't mention a gun in describing her experience, you—already having found out that the intruder was threatening the class with a semiautomatic weapon—might say, "Did the man have a weapon?" Then the child might reply, "Oh, yeah, and he put it to my head but I didn't want to tell you." If you rely only on the child's initial description of the event, you won't always find out the most crucial aspects and the most frightening moments in the child's experience. Don't be afraid to ask questions. However, be sure to use open-ended questions, and don't put your words in the child's mouth or you will inhibit the child from telling the story his or her way.

- *Telling a story through drawing:*   Ask the child to draw a picture of the event or simply to draw a picture of whatever comes to mind. Any picture will act as an entry into your discussion. After a trauma, drawings often relate to the event. The reference may be an oblique one, however, so be creative when looking at the drawing. For instance, following an earthquake, one boy drew a picture of a safe. I said, "Tell me about your picture." The drawing didn't represent the earthquake per se, but it made me aware of his feelings and of his need to find ways to secure his world.

  Another example comes from a debriefing I did with children following a hurricane. I put paper all around the walls and asked the children to paint a mural. I wanted them to be able to paint what had happened *around* them. The hurricane, with its howling winds and driving rain, had destroyed their homes and community, and I wanted the kids to be able to express that total devastation in a mural and not be confined to a small sheet of paper.

- *Telling a story through play:*   Very young children or those who don't have adequate verbal skills often express their feelings about trauma through play. They make toy cars go through endless collisions or make blocks fall down over and over or have one doll hit another doll. To tell a story through play, however, youngsters need appropriate toys. Consider carefully toy props for playing out the story. For instance, after a car crash, choose toy cars, an ambulance, and maybe a police car. If someone died in a hospital, you might want to have doctor and nurse dolls as well as a hospital bed and other appropriate props.

  Some debriefing games don't require props at all. At a debriefing following Hurricane Andrew, the very young children played London Bridge. They chose to play this game over and over.

- *Telling a story through role play:*   Some children relate their experiences more easily by acting them out rather than by using toy props. They may remember details through role play that they would not otherwise recall. You may want to role-play several different parts to get a full sense of what the child was feeling.

Have the child be the director. If the incident occurred at school, you can play the teacher, the principal, or one of the police officers who came to help, using the information you have gathered to make your representations as true as possible to what happened. You can say to the child, "What do you think the teacher saw and felt?"

Reversing roles can help jog the youngster's memory and make his or her impression of what happened more vivid to you. For instance, you might have played the role of the police officer in a reassuring way, but the child might play it in a gruff way that lets you know that the police officer's presence was more scary than comforting. To reverse roles, tell the child that you're going to pretend to be him and that he can take turns pretending to be the other people in the incident.

One or more of these techniques should allow the child to tell the story in her own way and to describe what she experienced during the event. If the youngster seems at a loss for how to begin, you can help get and keep the storytelling going by asking open-ended questions like these: Tell [or show] me what happened to you. What did you do then?

Pay attention to the details—the sights, sounds, and smells. The senses are aspects of the experience. Get an idea of who the child holds accountable. What fears does the child have?

The point of having the child tell the story is to allow her to discharge the feelings connected to the memories and experiences. Without this venting, the feelings leave a residue in the child's mind that will haunt her later. The experience of the event and the memory of the event can be different. The experience includes what is seen, smelled, heard, or touched. Although everything that is experienced is filed away in the brain, that doesn't mean that everything that happened becomes a retrievable memory. Although a person may not be able to recall every detail of an event, his or her subconscious mind will have taken it in and may respond unconsciously to certain stimuli in an aberrant way later on.

When people go through trauma, their senses take in the whole experience, but they are conscious of only a small part of what is going on. They have what we call tunnel vision. In a holdup, a person may consciously remember seeing the gun—"a big gun, a huge gun"—but not the person holding the gun. The victim's subconscious, however, has

likely taken in the whole event and can react later to cues that the conscious mind may not recall. If the robber was wearing a white uniform,
the victim may later feel unnerved when confronted by anyone in a similar
uniform or in a white garment, even though the victim has no conscious
recall of what the robber wore or looked like.

Any child who goes through a trauma may experience tunnel
vision. When you listen to the child's story, look for the omission of
important facts of which you are aware. Don't be afraid to bring them
up. Helping relate the trauma in full won't put ideas in the child's
head. What you will do is help the child vent fears and piece together
important parts of the event so that the memory and the unconscious
mind will be less likely to come back and haunt the child later.

Step III: Sharing the Child's Reaction
(Five to Fifteen Minutes)

The purpose of this step is to assist children in describing their reactions since the traumatic event and to understand that their responses
are normal. This is the part of the debriefing where your knowledge
of posttraumatic reactions is extremely important. Your knowledge
will help you elicit information from a child who is reluctant to talk
or who is having trouble describing what she is feeling.

You could open the discussion by asking, "How are you different
since the event?" or "What changes have you noticed in yourself since
the event?" (It's important to personalize the question, filling in
whatever the event was—for example, "since Uncle Charlie died" or
"since the hurricane destroyed our home.") If the youngster talks
readily, just sit back and listen. However, if the response is,
"Everything's fine," and you have seen behavior indicating that it's
not, or you otherwise suspect that it's not, don't just let it go. Continue to explore the child's reactions based on what you observe of
the child's behavior or by using examples of how children of the
same age commonly react after a trauma.

You might use the following questions to get a child to talk more
about reactions. (Choose the gender appropriate to your situation.)

- Boys/girls who had this experience (for example, had a parent
  die, been through a flood, witnessed a violent crime) sometimes
  feel scared, or they worry that it might happen again. Do you
  have those feelings?

- Sometimes boys/girls have a hard time going to sleep. I've noticed that you've been staying up later or asking to watch just one more program. Are you having difficulty falling asleep?
- Sometimes boys/girls have bad dreams. Do you?
- Sometimes boys/girls feel mad. Has this happened to you?

A child who reports feeling fine may in fact be fine, but if you open up the discussion with questions and sensitive probing, following the examples given earlier, you'll find out if there are fears, worries, anger, or even pleasure lurking below the surface. One four-year-old girl who seemed sanguine about her father's going into the hospital for minor shoulder surgery surprised her mother when asked if she had any thoughts about Daddy's operation. "Of course," she said. "Daddy's never coming home." If the mother hadn't taken the time to ask what was on her mind, she never would have known about her child's grim—and totally erroneous—conclusion.

Be specific when asking about fears that arise in the wake of a specific trauma. Say that other children who have been in car accidents are often afraid to get back into a car or that children who have been through earthquakes are sometimes afraid to be inside of buildings.

A child who doesn't have such feelings won't make them up to please you. This exercise lets children who have worries or problems and have been afraid to bring them up know that their feelings are normal and expected. It also helps them learn that there is nothing wrong with expressing these reactions. It's important for all people—adults and children—who have recently been through a divorce, the death of a loved one, or another trauma to be told that they're not crazy for having all these reactions even a couple of months after the event. Most individuals take a year or even longer to feel normal again. This is why such reassurance makes everyone, regardless of age or sex, feel less isolated and often less strange and more relaxed.

Step IV: Survival and Recovery
(Five to Ten Minutes)

One purpose of this step is to help the child understand that there are expected posttraumatic responses. For example, a child who was involved in an auto accident should be forewarned that cars may continue to be scary for a while but that the scariness will go away. It just takes time.

Another objective of this step is to teach the child a new set of coping skills. The coping skills youngsters have already developed to handle the minor frustrations of life, such as waiting for dessert until after dinner or learning to use words instead of hitting to settle a dispute, often won't help them come to terms with a death or a natural disaster. It is up to you to provide guidance to help your child develop new coping skills. Use these guidelines to make a plan to help the child cope with the aftermath of a trauma.

- *Explain that emotional reactions will decrease over time.* Tell the child that the anxiety and fears that he now feels will fade as time passes. Prepare the child by explaining that on the anniversary of the event or in situations very much like the trauma, the old feelings might arise again temporarily, but only for a short time and usually with less intensity. Preparedness reduces the intensity of the feelings and shortens the duration of the reactions.
- *Correct misconceptions.* At this point, correct any misconceptions that your child might have mentioned earlier. For example, a child who imagined that she yelled at the gunman might be worried that he will come after her for revenge. In the aftermath of a storm or earthquake, a child might worry that there won't be any food and that his family will starve. If one parent has died, a child might believe that the other parent might die, too. No matter how farfetched the concerns might seem, never ridicule the child for expressing them. To a child who doesn't have an adult's ability to put an experience in perspective, these concerns are very real. Treat them seriously, and explain why the concerns are unwarranted.
- *Make practical suggestions to help your child cope with fears.* One of the most important ways we cope with stress is coming up with solutions to individual problems that will ease the emotional burden of a crisis. Teaching children to think in this manner after a trauma gives them a skill that they will be able to use, not just in this situation, but in any stressful event.

Here are some practical suggestions that you can use or adapt to your situation:

- Kids who experienced an earthquake asked to take heavy objects off of the shelves near their beds and store them near the floor so that they wouldn't be hurt by things falling off the shelves.

- A child who was moving from his home as a result of a divorce asked to go back into his room once the movers had finished taking his belongings so he could put his name and an epitaph in the corner of the closet. This made him feel as if his life with his family intact wasn't being wiped out forever.

- When a girl was traumatized because a classmate had been abducted from her home and killed, her mother suggested that she write to the victim's mother and tell her how fondly she remembered her classmate and how badly she felt about what happened. It worked.

- If a child is having bad dreams, make a dream catcher. This Native American ornament is often made with a string web woven onto a wooden circle. The web has a hole in it through which the good dreams pass, but the bad dreams get caught in the web. Dream catcher kits are available in some hobby stores, but yours doesn't have to be exactly like those from the Native American tradition. You can build one out of anything you have as long as it can hang near the pillow and "catch" bad dreams.

- Another way to handle bad dreams is to consciously decide to dream differently. At bedtime, help the child come up with things that he wants to dream about other than the subject of his nightmares.

- Another tack to take with recurrent bad dreams is to imagine a different ending. If a child has survived a car crash and keeps dreaming about the moment of impact, have her imagine Superman swooping down at the scene of the accident and carrying the car off to safety. Though dreams are not the stuff of the conscious mind, you'll be surprised how much control your child can have over them.

- If a child is anxious that the event will happen again with the same terrible results, you can help him by suggesting that he think of things that he could do so that the outcome would be different. Maybe he could move his bed to a safer place or have the family buy a supply of canned food and water so that they won't be suddenly without those necessities in the event of a natural disaster.

- If a child is fearful that she might be separated from her family if another natural disaster occurs, come up with a plan for getting the family together from jobs and schools in the event of an emergency. Designate an out-of-town relative who will serve as a contact person. Have your child carry telephone change in a change purse if she is concerned about not being able to reach you.

Ask the child what he can do—with your help if necessary—to make himself feel less vulnerable in the future. What can he do to either make the event less likely (kidnapping) or make the danger less likely if the event cannot be controlled (natural disaster)? Anything you can suggest that makes the child feel safe and secure is suitable.

* *Help the child remember something good or funny that happened.* Here you'll focus on rising above adversity. The point is to help your child see how resilient the human spirit is, how even in the most difficult circumstances, people find the strength to rise to the occasion. Children show that resilience, too, in their efforts to come to terms with their feelings and go on with their lives.

  Talk with your child about the heroism of the people involved in the incident, whether they are police officers, doctors, or relief workers. Who can forget the pictures of the firefighters sifting through the rubble of Oklahoma City or the firefighter carrying the child in his arms?

  What heroic efforts have others made in the midst of this event? How has your child been heroic in his or her efforts to get over the trauma? Talk about how it is brave to face up to the fears and other feelings that the child talked about in the debriefing. Then you can go on to discuss how it is brave that your child is trying to go on with his or her life by going back to school or playing with friends.

HELP YOURSELF FIRST

When you take a plane trip, the flight attendant, in reviewing the instructions for an emergency, always says to put your own oxygen mask on first before putting one on your child so that you'll be lucid and able to help. The same is true for debriefing after a trauma. Before you begin to help your child, you need to help yourself.

It might not be possible for you to conduct the debriefing yourself. Adults are not immune to the effects of a trauma. They feel distraught, and that's perfectly normal. However, grown-ups have the added burden of knowing that children rely on them even when they're too busy and too overwrought to offer emotional support. Though you try to be supportive, you may find yourself being short-tempered and less patient than you usually are. At such times, it's a good idea to call on family or friends to help out and even to debrief your child for you. They can give the child the attention he or she needs while you grapple with your emotions and with getting life back to normal. You can talk to your child later about the trauma and his or her experience when you are feeling more able.

Sometimes you may just need some time to regain your emotional footing before you help your child. The following are some useful ways to regain your equilibrium:

- *Recognize that you are under great stress and that you have to take extra good care of yourself.* Make sure that your eating and sleeping habits are as near to normal as possible. Give yourself time out from dealing with the aftermath of the trauma. The break will give you strength to continue.
- *Take steps to help lower stress for yourself and your children.* Plan some pleasant activities when you're feeling good. A board game, a home movie with popcorn, or a family hike are some ideas.
- *Remember that no one is to blame.* You may find yourself more irritable than normal and quicker to fight with your partner and children. Remember that being thin-skinned and blaming others is a normal reaction to trauma. To stop this tendency, take a few moments alone to cool off. A brisk walk or a long, warm bath can help.
- *Talk about your feelings with your partner, friends, a health professional, or a member of the clergy.* Most people feel relieved when they have a chance to express their regrets and fears.
- *Talk about plans to handle future crises.* You'll feel stronger and more secure.
- *Keep a journal.* Writing about what you are going through and what you are feeling often helps.
- *Talk about the funny and good things that happened during the crisis.* Yes, there are always some.

PREPARING YOUR CHILD
FOR DEBRIEFING

It's important to tell your child what you are going to do and why. You might say, "I know a bad thing happened to you. I can't make that bad thing go away, but I know that talking about what happened might make it easier for you to understand what occurred, why it happened, and how you can feel safer." You'll have to choose words that are appropriate to the child's age, but the message you want to get across is that you are going to talk about the trauma and that afterward you think the child will feel better.

HOW TO USE THE
DEBRIEFING METHOD

Here's an example of how you can use a debriefing to reach out to a child after a trauma.

> Recently, a woman came to my office with her two-and-a-half-year-old daughter, both of whom had witnessed the murder of the father two weeks previously. The mother was concerned because the child kept asking for her father and she'd become clingy at bedtime and temperamental during the day.
>
> When I asked the mother to tell me what had happened, the little girl put her finger to her lips and said, "Shhh, shhh." The mother dismissed her, saying, "Oh, she always does that," and then told me her story.
>
> She had been awakened in the middle of the night by the sound of her husband's gasp from the living room. When she came out of the bedroom, she saw two men standing near him. One of them had a gun. The intruders ordered her to get her children and come into the living room. She went into her daughter's room and gathered her in her arms with the intention of trying to run out of the apartment. She came back into the living room and started toward the door. The intruders

told her to stop. Her husband struggled with the gunman, and the man shot him.

The mother didn't know if she should say anything to her daughter about what they had witnessed. If something had to be said to the child, she wanted me to do it. I started to talk to the child. I said, "Tell me what happened to you." The child said, "They shot my Daddy." I said, "What happened then?" The mother interrupted me at every other word, admonishing me not to use words like *blood* or *dead* because she didn't like those words to be used around her daughter, even though she believed that the child didn't understand them.

Now I understood why the child had hushed everyone when the subject of her father's murder came up. The mother, in an effort to protect her daughter, was constantly censoring what was said to her. She thought that much of the event was beyond the girl's comprehension and had made little impression on her. "She's little," the mother said. "She'll miss her father, but she won't remember what happened." The mother believed that the less said about the incident in front of the girl, the better. She didn't want to put any frightening ideas in her head. She believed that the event would recede into the foggy memories of childhood.

I was able to persuade the mother to let me continue, and I encouraged her daughter to go on with her story by asking her what else she'd seen. She replied, "I saw red on his shirt, and then Mommy kissed him."

When she finished her story, we talked about the fact that her father wasn't coming home. "Your daddy is not in the hospital," I said. "He's dead. He can't come home. Dead means that he can't breathe, eat, or sleep anymore."

I was helping her understand that there was a word that explained why her father didn't come home. He had died, so he can't come home. It's not because he doesn't want to or that he doesn't care. He can't.

We then talked about the red on her father's shirt. I said, "The red was blood from where the bullet hurt your daddy. It was the bullet that made your daddy dead." Also, I told her that her mother hadn't been kissing her father, but trying to help him breathe. I wanted her to understand that her mother hadn't just stood by and let her husband die; she had tried to keep him alive. Now what she had seen made more sense. Now she had the words to describe what happened.

As she told her story, the child walked around my office, took paper clips off of my desk, and dropped them behind the radiator. Then she looked underneath to see if they were there. The mother wanted her to stop messing up my office. I explained to her that the child was making the paper clips go away. She was playing out her father's absence, which she didn't understand.

I made some suggestions to the mother that would help her daughter come to terms with her father's death. First, I told her to make a photo album of the daughter's favorite pictures of Daddy and the family. Second, I suggested that the daughter spend more time with her grandfather. Third, I urged the mother to make some time for herself so that she would feel less stressed. Finally, I reminded the mother that her daughter would need the story told many times because she was very young and easily confused.

Children do not easily forget traumatic situations. Though small children may be limited in their ability to describe what they experienced and how they feel, they are no less aware than adults when something unusual and horrifying happens. The little girl I saw may not have known the word for blood, but surely she was affected by the blood running from her father's body and by the bloody stains on the couch and carpet. They were vivid reminders of the brutal shooting of her father. Censoring what was said in front of her would not remove the bloody images from her mind. In fact, creating a veil of silence around a traumatic experience often harms more than helps a child because the child does not have the opportunity to explore the memory.

Much as they might like, concerned adults cannot undo the trauma. Pretending that the death, divorce, or hurricane did not happen does not make it any less real. Adults can, however, help integrate the event into the child's life in such a way that it has some positive rather than only negative effects. By listening to traumatized children, the debriefer can dispel the misconceptions and assuage the guilt and fear that children feel in the wake of a traumatic experience.

Debriefing can also interrupt the development of posttraumatic stress disorder (see Chapter 2) by helping children sort through their feelings and find ways to restore a sense of order and security in the world.

Remember, however, to consult a professional if your child's distress seems especially acute or if it persists or increases after the debriefing.

The following chapters offer information about specific kinds of traumatic situations and how the debriefing method can be applied in each of those situations. However, the debriefing method outlined in this chapter may be used not only in the situations described in the following chapters, but with appropriate modifications in the wake of any traumatic event that a child might experience.

PART TWO

WORKING THROUGH TRAUMATIC EVENTS

5

DEATH

Coping with Loss

Like many adults, you may be unsure about how to approach the subject of death with a young person, whether it's the death of a close relative, a friend, or a pet. To help your child, you first need to know how children react to death and how they mourn. You can use this information in the debriefing process, which will help the child cope with the loss.

WHAT YOU SHOULD KNOW
ABOUT DEATH

There is a controversy among child counselors about whether the death of a significant person is traumatic to a child. Some mental health professionals believe that the loss of a significant person—whether by abandonment or actual death—is certainly a trauma. Others in the field feel that the death of someone close to a child is traumatic only if it occurs in a sudden or violent way. If a mother is murdered, it is a traumatic experience. However, if she dies in the hospital after a long illness, it is sad but not necessarily traumatic.

I feel that the answer to this controversy lies somewhere between these two extremes. I believe that a loss of a significant person in a child's life is traumatic. Even if the loss was expected by adults, it is an unexpected event in the life of a child. Young people imagine and expect that those who are close to them will be around throughout their young lives and always.

I also believe, however, that some deaths are more traumatic than others. It is more traumatic for a child to lose a primary caregiver than it is to lose a great-grandmother whom the child visited a few times in the nursing home. It is more traumatic for a youngster to see his mother crushed to death in a car crash than it is to watch her die peacefully in her bed at home after a long illness. It is important to recognize the differences in degree of trauma because children cannot get on with the normal process of mourning unless they first deal with their feelings about the traumatic aspect of a death.

HOW CHILDREN REACT TO DEATH

Adults know that death is irreversible, universal, and inevitable. Children gradually develop the ability to understand these abstract qualities as they mature.

Preschoolers (Ages Two to Five)

Preschool children do not understand the concept of forever, nor can they grasp such concepts as universality or inevitability. An hour after you finish a long explanation about Daddy being dead, these youngsters are likely to ask, "When's Daddy coming home?" These young girls and boys live in a cartoon world. Wile E. Coyote gets smooshed but comes back in the next minute.

To help them grasp the concept of death, preschool children need concrete information about what dying means, and they need to hear it over and over again. Here are some suggestions to help you explain death to these young children:

- *Use only one word for death.*   The words *dying* and *dead* have no meaning to preschoolers. If you use *died* in one sentence and *dead* in the next, the youngster will think you are talking about two different things. Pick one word to refer to the event, and stick with it. Otherwise, you'll only confuse the child.
- *Explain what being dead means.*   When you tell a preschooler that someone has died, you need to explain what that means. You can say, for instance, "Daddy is dead. He can't eat. He can't breathe. He can't play. He can't come home. Dead is when you

can no longer do those things." The first and even the second time, this explanation won't necessarily stop a young child from coming back an hour later and asking, "When is Daddy coming home?" You have to repeat what you've said over and over.

- *Describe what the deceased can no longer do.* Preschoolers also don't understand when you say, "Daddy was sick and had a bad heart." They don't understand the nature of illness or the sickness of a body part. Again, it's better to describe what Daddy can no longer do to help a child of this age understand the terminal nature of death.
- *Be honest about death.* You're not protecting a young child by telling her that the person who has died is sleeping forever. You'll only confuse the child and perhaps even create a worry that she also may go to sleep and never wake.

School-Age Children (Ages Six to Twelve)

Children at the younger end of this age group, say between six and eight, have some sense that death is irreversible, but they still believe that death occurs only to old people. Grandpa died because he was old. This reasoning leads to questions like, "Mom, are you old yet?" or "Dad, when will you be old?" which have less to do with age and more to do with susceptibility to dying. Younger school-age children don't understand yet the universality or the inevitability of death.

However, around the age of nine, school-age children's reasoning ability develops to the point where they can grasp that death is permanent and that it happens to young and old alike. They understand that death is irreversible and inevitable, but they still believe that it only happens to other people.

Teenagers (Ages Thirteen to Eighteen)

Teens recognize all aspects of death—its irreversibility, universality, and inevitability. They differ from grown-ups, however, in that they are fascinated by death. Death is romanticized in the music they hear and in the books they read. Adolescents also challenge death by driving fast, experimenting with drugs, and taking other unnecessary risks.

Death is fascinating to teens because it is so threatening to them. The central developmental task of this age group is to define an identity

that is separate from the family. Therefore, teens are very preoccupied with how they look because they want to be attractive to and
accepted by their peers. They are also concerned about what they
will be and what they will do in life. For a teen, death signifies the
loss of attractiveness, independence, and strength forever. Death
interrupts life and destroys goals at a time when teens are only beginning to figure out what they want to be and what they want to
attain. One way for teens to fight back against this awesome force is
by doing dangerous things, which allows them to challenge death,
get close to it, and then escape it or beat it.

HOW CHILDREN MOURN

In addition to recognizing that the death of someone close is traumatic for children, adults who are helping a child cope with a death
need to understand how children mourn.

Grieving versus Mourning

Grieving and mourning follow the death of a loved one. Grief refers to
the initial period of intense sadness and loss following the death of a
significant other. Mourning begins when we move beyond the initial
stage of grief. It ends when we incorporate the loss into our life.

These two phases are recognized in many religious rituals surrounding death. For instance, in the Jewish religion, you "sit shiva"
for seven days following the death. That's the period when you grieve.
Then you go through a period of mourning that is expected to last a
year. The unveiling of the deceased's tombstone at the end of the
year marks the end of the period of mourning. In Christianity, the
wake following the death is the period of grieving. Survivors then
wear black for a year, which is the traditional period of mourning in
this religion, also.

The Stages of Mourning

The emotional responses experienced by children and adults during
the mourning process are sadness, denial, guilt, anger, shame or stigma,

and finally, acceptance. In children, there is also an overlay of feeling stigmatized or shamed. Children may feel odd and different from their peers as a result of a death.

The mourning process is not linear in children as it is in adults. For children, there is no beginning, middle, and end. Rather, the process is repeated as the child grows older and understands the death from a more mature perspective. Children can mourn in bits and pieces. Long periods can pass when their mourning appears to be over. Then some event precipitates a reemergence of the mourning cycle. If a school-age girl's mother dies in a car crash, she will mourn at that time for the loss. However, she's likely to go through the process again as a teenager when she reaches milestones like graduation. She'll mourn again at the time of her marriage when her mother isn't there to help her pick out her dress and play the traditional maternal role during that important life event. Finally, she's likely to go through another mourning period when she has her own children and is unable to go to her mother for advice or when she thinks of how she lost her own mother when she was just a child.

Sadness

A period of sadness almost always accompanies a major loss. It is not unusual for children to show signs of depression at times. A child may withdraw from friends, ignore toys, and experience school performance problems following the death of a loved person. These are "normal" symptoms of depression following a death. You should see less and less of these symptoms over time.

The pain of the loss can be so great, however, that a child may express wishes to "not wake up" or to "go to heaven." Young children do not understand the finality of death, so you will need to tell them what happened many times. If your child seems especially sad and preoccupied with death, begins to take unnecessary risks, or gives away belongings, consult a professional immediately.

Denial

Everyone reacts to a death with an initial sense of disbelief. For children, blocking out the unpleasant is natural. Particularly for young children, it's very easy to live in the pretend. Young children have a limited capacity to tolerate emotional distress. You might see them appear grief stricken one minute and off riding a bicycle as if nothing happened the next because children can't tolerate feeling so badly.

When confronted with something they find overwhelmingly unpleasant, children very easily step out of the real world into one they find more acceptable.

Of course, you don't want a youngster to escape into a fantasy all of the time. Boys and girls have to live in the real world, too. You can help children get through the denial stage by reminiscing about the deceased. The more they know about the person and the death, the more real the loss is for them. However, when talking about the death, avoid horrific details if the child hasn't been exposed to them already.

Reminiscing about the deceased in healthier times is particularly important when the person who dies is the parent of the same sex as the child. Part of the normal development of a child is to form an identification with the same-sex parent. If the last image of the parent was a horrible one, the child may fear that if he identifies with the parent, he'll also meet a traumatic ending. The result is that the normal developmental process of identification with the same-sex parent is interrupted.

Though a period of denial is expected, it is also anticipated that a child will move on to the next stage of mourning within a given period of time. That time is anywhere from a few days to a few months, but most of us have a sense of when the period of denial should be over. Think of a woman who loses her spouse. If she refers to him in the present tense during the first week or so after the death, you'd consider that normal. However, if she's still talking about him in the here and now several months after the funeral, you'd begin to wonder if she was all right.

The same is true for school-age and teenage children. Young school-age children may spend more time denying a death than teenagers, but after a certain point, you'd even expect a child in this age group to grasp that a person is dead. Preschoolers, however, will continue to have difficulty with the issue of permanence until they mature enough to understand that some things are forever. If the child seems stuck in denial, you'll want to take some steps to help. It is probably a good idea to consult a professional if the denial stage persists.

Guilt

The death of a loved one accentuates issues of responsibility. This is especially true if the death occurred through violent means rather than through natural causes. As adults, we often go over the scene in our minds, endlessly looking for ways in which we could have prevented the death: If only we had . . .

Children can have similar feelings of guilt following a death. They may believe that they caused the death or may feel guilty for not preventing the death. A young child who, in a fit of pique, shouts, "I hate you, Daddy," will feel guilty if his father dies suddenly thereafter. If a teenager commits suicide after expressing her unhappiness to a friend, the friend may feel as if she should have known enough to intervene, that she should have picked up on the depth of the unhappiness and prevented the suicide.

If children don't explore their guilty feelings after a death, those feelings will distort how they remember and feel about the deceased and about themselves. If children don't have an opportunity to straighten out their misplaced sense of accountability, they may develop guilt fantasies—that is, fears that they will be harmed in some way for their role in the death.

For instance, a four-year-old boy who had seen his father murdered by intruders told me that he had shouted at the men to stop and that if only he had shouted louder, maybe they would have gone away and then his father would be alive. In fact, he hadn't shouted at all, according to his mother, but his guilt about not doing something to protect his father made this fantasy real. To help him understand that he wasn't responsible, I said, "You know, even a grown-up couldn't have done anything to help your father. The men had guns, and yelling wouldn't have stopped them. Besides, you're only a little boy, and it's not your place to protect a grown-up. No one would expect you to do that."

Anger

In adulthood, the anger stage of mourning often takes the shape of anger at the deceased for abandoning the survivors. A wife shouts in anger at her husband for leaving her alone for the rest of her life.

In childhood, the anger that arises during the period of mourning comes from an additional source. Children find the emotions they feel following a death to be confusing and disorienting. They don't understand what's going on inside of them. Why are they feeling insecure? Why are they uncomfortable? Why are the adults around them crying and upset? Children often respond to these overwhelming feelings in the only way they know how, which is to act out and

be disruptive. Young boys, especially, can show their confusion by
being angry and disruptive. At the same time, however, children feel
guilty for acting out. They know that they're annoying the adults
around them, and the grown-ups seem upset enough already. Kids
just can't help themselves.

If you can keep in mind where the anger and disruptive behavior
are coming from, you'll be much more able to respond sympatheti-
cally rather than be angry. When you are distraught over the loss of
a loved one, it is very difficult to deal with the petty arguments that
crop up between siblings or with their bad behavior. It is easy to start
yelling, "Stop it! You're driving me crazy." However, you'll go a lot
farther in defusing the anger and preventing future outbursts if you
can count to ten and respond instead by saying, "Maybe you're feeling angry because everyone is upset and nothing is the way it normally is. Maybe this is the way you're letting me know how you feel,
by getting angry. Let's see what we can do to get things back to normal
for you."

Shame or Stigma

Where adults derive comfort from condolences, expressions of concern, and the opportunity these offer to talk about their feelings of
grief, children dread this process. Children want to be just like other
kids their own age. They don't want to be seen as being different
because they don't have a father or because their sister died in a car
crash. They don't want to feel different from their peers because of
the loss of someone dear, and they don't want to be pitied. When the
teacher announces to the class that Johnny is back after the funeral
of his dad and asks the class to take a minute to express its sympathy,
Johnny may feel like shrinking under his desk instead of experiencing some solace from the attention.

Children also feel both stigmatized and excluded on occasions
when the deceased is needed to play a role in the child's life. For
instance, a young boy who has been playing in Little League for
several years may feel that he can't be a part of the league anymore
because he no longer has a father to take him to the games or to
volunteer as coach—regardless of whether this is true.

Children feel particularly shamed if the death attains notoriety in
the media or if there is a trial at which they have to testify. In such
situations, you should protect your child from unnecessary media
exposure and consult with law enforcement and court personnel to

try to make appropriate arrangements to minimize any adverse effects on your child.

Children who may not be comforted by grown-up expressions of condolence may find solace in a group of peers who have also experienced a death. In this group, they fit in. They no longer feel stigmatized. Some schools and community centers offer brief (six- to eight-week) focus groups for bereaved children to help them explore their feelings about what happened and to discuss how they will get their lives back to normal.

Acceptance

In adults, the final stage of the mourning cycle is acceptance. At this point, they are able to release themselves from the love and devotion they had for the deceased and commit themselves to another person.

Children, however, rarely reach this stage. They need to preserve the image of and the relationship with the deceased loved one. They hold onto the affection for and attachment to the person in order to have that person's presence in their lives as they go through the milestones of growing up. Once they grow up and they no longer need that attachment, they will reach the acceptance stage.

DEBRIEFING FOR DEATH

To tailor a debriefing for death, you need to consider where the child is in the mourning cycle and how much the child can understand.

For young children, in particular, part or all of the debriefing following a death will probably have to be repeated several times. Preschoolers and young school-age children don't understand the concept of death, and you will have to explain what happened more than once. Children will also need to repeat parts of the debriefing as they reach a more mature understanding of death and once again have to come to terms with the impact of the loss of a significant person.

Don't wait for an ideal time or circumstance to begin talking to your child about the death. After a loved one has died, there often isn't a good time to talk about the death. Even if you are comfortable with the subject, it's not a pleasant thing to do. Your own feelings of grief will be obvious, and because of all of the activity surrounding the funeral plans, you're likely to be rushed. It's generally better to be quick and truthful when telling a child rather than wait until a perfect moment to bring it up. The youngster may be upset, but at least she will know what is going on around her. Remember, however, if you are too overwrought, have someone else talk to your child for you.

Step I: Preparing Yourself

You can prepare yourself by thinking or writing about your own feelings about death. This exercise will help you become comfortable with talking about death with your child. Consider the following:

- The first death of a loved one that you experienced
- The first funeral you attended
- How you felt at the funeral

You don't need to be stoic when talking about the death of a loved one to a child. It's all right to be sad and even to cry, though if your grief is out of control, it's better to have someone else conduct the debriefing. By showing emotion yourself, you give the child permission to show emotion, too.

If the youngster seems upset at seeing you sad, you can say something like, "Sad things like this make me cry, and when I cry, I like to get hugs." This explanation will make the child less frightened when she sees you cry and will also make her feel better about her own tears. You also give the child something to do when she sees you upset so she won't feel so helpless.

Another important part of preparation is finding out how much of the process of death the child observed and what that experience was like. Remember that at this stage of the debriefing process, you are talking only with others and not yet with your child. Did the child see the person die? Was it a peaceful passing or a violent one? Was the person at home or in the hospital? It's an added trauma for a child to see a loved person who has become emaciated and attached to intravenous lines and tubes in the hospital or for the child to see someone gravely injured at the site of an automobile accident.

Be prepared as well to discuss medical information with the child. He may ask, "Did he suffer?" or, if an illness is involved, "Will I get it, too?" Older children may ask more sophisticated questions about a fatal disease and how it caused the person to die.

Religion often provides great support and solace to grown-ups when a death takes place, and it can be helpful to children, too. However, when you are preparing to talk to a child, you should be aware that there are some common explanations for death that may cause more harm than good. In general, avoid the following explanations of death:

- Don't say that God loved your father so He took him to heaven, because children perceive this to mean that they didn't love their father enough. If they had, God wouldn't have taken him.
- Don't say that it was God's plan for the person to die, because children will worry that God might have a plan for them, too.
- Don't say that God answers all prayers, because children might feel that they didn't pray hard enough or might be disappointed when their prayers to get the deceased back aren't answered.

Step II: Having the Child Tell the Story

To help the child begin to talk about the experience, you might ask the following questions:

- What happened to the person who died?
- Where were you when you first heard about what happened?
- What did you do when you first heard about the death?

Very young children are bound to be confused about the concept of death, and you can clarify what they heard and saw. For instance, when a young child says, "My mommy died," one minute and then asks, "When is Mommy coming back?" a few minutes later, you can help the little one grasp the finality of death by saying, "You know, your mommy died. She can't come back. She can't move or breathe or eat or play. She can't help you anymore now that she's dead, but I can help you and so can your daddy and all of the other people who love you."

Another way to reach young children is to use puppets and have a pretend conversation between the child and the deceased person. The child can ask the deceased what happened, and you can answer for the person who passed away. Without going into gory explanations, you can give the child details about what happened that will make the death more real to her. Some of the things you might discuss are how old the person was; the last thing he or she did; how the person died; what the person died of; where the person was when he or she died; and who was with the person at the death.

If the youngster refuses to talk with you or leaves the room when anyone talks about the deceased, you might suspect that the child is lingering in the denial stage of grief. You might say, "I notice that you leave the room whenever anyone talks about Daddy." You can empathize with the youngster about how painful it is to lose someone. "Maybe it hurts too much to hear people talking about Daddy, but it will hurt less and less as time goes on." Reassure the child by saying, "I love you," and "You will be all right. It will just take time."

If the funeral has taken place by the time you debrief the child, you'll want to ask about the details of the youngster's experience. The child might report, for instance, that "Grandma cried, but Daddy helped her." You might ask about these topics:

- Who was at the funeral or how many people were there
- What the child and the relatives wore
- Where the service took place
- How the grown-ups and kids reacted
- How the child felt about the funeral
- If the child went to the cemetery, describe that experience

Girls and boys sometimes get stuck in the denial stage of mourning when the last memories of the deceased are too painful to recall. They turn away from those memories. They do not want to think or talk about the deceased because it brings up those awful final images. Yet a basic factor in progressing through the cycle of mourning is remembering and reminiscing about the deceased. One of the things you need to do to help the child over this impediment is to talk about the gruesome details. There's no need to add more details to what the child already knows, nor should you sensationalize or linger on gory descriptions. Conversely, you should not try to minimize the effect of the child's having seen a significant person in terrible condition. What helps is acknowledging how horrifying some of these memories must be and helping the child articulate the experience.

Some of the memories that would be good to bring up include

what the hospital or site of the accident looked or smelled like; what the hospital food smelled or tasted like; what unusual noises the child associates with the hospital or the accident; how the dying person looked and felt. You might say something like, "How frightening it must have been to see your father so thin with all of his hair gone and hooked up to all of those monitors. It's no wonder that you didn't want to see him or hug and kiss him."

In the case of suicide, many adults are afraid to be frank with children about the cause of death. However, it's best to tell the truth because children's imaginings can often be worse than reality. You don't have to go into gruesome details. Saying something simple is best, for instance, "Your brother had an illness in his mind that made him very sick. That's why he took his life. It had nothing to do with you or anyone else. You didn't do anything to cause your brother's death, nor could you have done anything to prevent it."

Step III: Sharing the Child's Reaction

When you talk to the child about what life has been like since the death of a loved one, help her think of ways to handle the emotions that commonly arise. If a child says that she is very angry, you might say, "Lots of children are angry when their Daddy dies. You might feel better if you found a way to let go of some of those angry feelings. Some kids find that it helps to run or ride a bicycle when they're feeling angry. Others write about how mad they are to get rid of some of the anger. You might even want to make a tape recording telling Daddy how angry you are about his death."

On the other hand, if a child says that he has been feeling sad and crying all the time since a loved one died, you can help him by saying, "I feel sad and miss Mommy, too. What thoughts make you sad?" The child might say that every night, Mommy would read a story before bedtime. Then you can respond, "I can see why you're sad about that and miss that. Maybe I can help by reading you a story the same way. We'll keep a picture of Mommy here while we're looking at the book so she feels close, too. I love you, honey, and I want you to know that you won't hurt so badly as time goes on. The sadness will go away."

Some situations involving the death of a loved one or a pet may bring about feelings of guilt in a child. Do not dismiss or minimize the child's expressions of guilt, responsibility, or remorse. Hear the child out. Sometimes, there are real reasons for these feelings. I can recall a situation in which an eight-year-old was very distressed because he had overmedicated his turtle, and the turtle had died. The boy needed the opportunity to talk about his guilt and remorse. On the other hand, sometimes the feeling of responsibility is not valid. Remember, very young children don't understand that there is not a cause-and-effect relationship between all events. A very young child needs to be reassured that her yelling did not cause the car accident that occurred later that day. Older children and teenagers can also feel responsible unnecessarily. For example, if a friend of your teenager commits suicide, your teenager might say, "I feel like it is my fault that Marie killed herself. She told me she was upset and mad, and I didn't do anything." You can appropriately respond, "When someone kills herself, everyone who knew the person feels a little guilty. But we have no way of knowing what's in someone else's mind. You couldn't have known Marie was going to kill herself. When someone kills herself, it's because her mind is sick. It's not your fault. Let's think about what we can do to make it easier for kids to get help if they should feel like Marie."

When a close family member dies, especially a parent or sibling, children often react with shame. If your child tells you that he doesn't know what to say or that he just wants to hide when kids come up to him in school and either punch his arm or cry, you can help your child feel less shame by telling him, "Kids who have someone close to them die are often embarrassed. The attention will stop soon. You will get more comfortable saying things like, 'Thanks for your concern. We're doing okay.' It just takes time."

Many children are confused when they see adults laughing and apparently feeling happy soon after the funeral. They wonder why everyone isn't crying all of the time. It's good to help children understand that one way people help the very bereaved—the people closest to the deceased—is to reminisce and remember funny and good things about the deceased. That's one way that grieving people get a break from the pain they're suffering. It also serves to remind the bereaved that they will not always feel such pain but will at some point come to accept the death and be able to enjoy the memories of the loved person who died.

Step IV: Survival and Recovery

If the funeral has not yet taken place, this is the time to tell your child about the funeral plans. If the debriefing follows the funeral, you can talk about what the new household routines will be.

If the funeral has not taken place, you'll want to prepare the children for the event. Help them understand the following:

- What the ritual will be like
- Whether they will see or touch the body
- What the body will feel, smell, and look like
- What people will be doing (crying, giggling because they're nervous, even though nothing funny is happening)
- What is likely to be said, and what a eulogy is
- What the hearse looks like
- How the cars will form a procession with lights on

If the child will be at the gravesite, talk about the rituals of burying. Will the child be expected to throw dirt on the coffin or watch the coffin being lowered into the ground? Older children can even be included in the planning of the funeral.

Children from the age of three and up, in my opinion, are able to attend a funeral. However, never force a child to go. You can explain what will happen and why you think the youngster should go, but if she steadfastly refuses, it's best to let it be.

If the child will be attending the funeral, have someone available who will be able to take the child away from time to time to take a break from the intense emotional situation or who can take the child home if the funeral is just too overwhelming for the little one.

With older children, you might want to talk about making a "personal memorial" for the deceased. Talk about tombstones and what they represent, and ask the child what she would put as an epitaph on the deceased's tombstone. It probably won't be what a grown-up would choose, but something like, "In memory of Tommy, who could swim better than anybody." You can also suggest that the child draw a picture to put on the "tombstone." Children might want to write a short eulogy to express their feelings about the deceased. Older children should be offered the opportunity to read their eulogy if they wish or to have it read on their behalf.

After the funeral has taken place, you'll need to take the time to explain to your child what changes, if any, will occur in his or her lifestyle and when things will settle back into a routine. Will there be a new baby-sitter or a whole new day-care situation? If a parent has died, who will take over the caregiving that the parent offered the child?

Children will also want to know how their future will be affected. What about summer vacations? Will you still visit your same favorite place? Will you not go at all during the year of mourning? This may be the farthest thing from your mind as you try to cope from one day to the next, but you need to look ahead to help assuage your child's anxieties about this yawning void in his or her life.

Children will probably return to school in a week or two, depending on the level of trauma they have suffered as a result of the death. They will dread the first few days, when everyone focuses attention on their loss, and they'll need to prepare what they will say to other children and to the teacher immediately on their return. Rehearse their responses with them.

Children will also run into stumbling blocks later on during awkward moments when the absence of the loved one is brought to light again. If a parent has died, these sticky situations arise on Mother's or Father's Day, on special occasions when parents are expected, such as Parents' Night, and during celebrations and school plays that parents usually attend. They also crop up when phone calls come in for the deceased several months down the road.

Help children anticipate these situations, and imagine how they will feel. What could the child say to get past the awkward moment as quickly as possible? These trying times after the funeral offer an opportunity to reiterate to the child that, even though sad times will come up now and again, life will go on without the deceased, and the sad times won't feel so sad later. It just takes time to heal. You will need to say this over and over to the child.

A child who persists in believing that the dead person will be returning needs help grasping the finality of death in concrete ways. One thing you can do is to take a nature walk and talk about death in nature—for example, in plants and trees. Another more direct method is to read to the child a book about death. (You'll find a suggested reading list in Appendix 3.) Make sure, however, that you read the book to yourself first to make sure that you agree with the presentation of death.

DEATH AT A DISTANCE

Children are more affected than adults by the deaths of people they don't know well, such as a classmate, a classmate's parent, or a hero. Don't minimize their feelings. Instead, go through the steps of the debriefing as they apply. Have them write a memorial or send a card to the bereaved. The distress may seem overblown to you, but it's very real to the child who is experiencing it.

DEATH OF A PET

The death of a pet offers a perfect opportunity to talk about what dying means and to explore the child's feelings about death. Some children shrug off the death of a pet and want a new one the next day, but others are truly grief stricken at the loss. Let the child know how the pet died, and if it's reasonable, offer to have a burial service in the backyard or park. The child can plan the pet's funeral with you and make a memorial to it if he or she wants.

6

ABUSE

The Ultimate Betrayal

I f a child has been abused physically or sexually, or if a child has been witness to spousal abuse, it is likely that the child will experience posttraumatic acute-stress reactions. If the abuse has been going on for a long time, the child is likely to experience the symptoms of PTSD. In this chapter, you'll find the information you need to reach out and begin the healing process.

WHAT YOU SHOULD KNOW
ABOUT ABUSE

If you have recently learned that your child was abused, you are likely to be horrified and bewildered by the circumstances. Let me assure you that your reaction is normal. You too are probably feeling the symptoms of a posttraumatic acute-stress reaction. If you find yourself thinking; "I'm the parent. I'm supposed to protect my child and I didn't," focus instead on feeling secure that you are now doing what is needed to help the child.

Physical Abuse

Child physical abuse covers a range of behaviors, from too forceful or too frequent "spankings" to punishments that include broken bones, burns, and, in extreme cases, death. We know the following about families in which physical abuse occurs.

61

- Parents who physically abuse their children often were abused as children themselves.
- Abusive parents, in many cases, are teenagers, single, and poor.
- Parents who abuse children often have substance-abuse problems.
- Stepparents are more likely to be abusive than biological parents.

Sexual Abuse

Here are some of the facts about sexual abuse that you should keep in mind:

- Child molesters are rarely disheveled, evil-looking strangers who would scare away any child. More often, they are family members, neighbors, scout leaders, or other trusted, known individuals who hold good jobs and appear to be upstanding members of the community.
- An estimated 16 to 35 percent of girls and 4 to 9 percent of boys under the age of eighteen are or have been sexually abused. Half of the victims are under twelve years of age. Statistically, sexual abuse begins when the child is between four and twelve years of age, with peaks at ages four and nine. In girls under the age of twelve or thirteen, the abuse rarely includes sexual intercourse.
- Sexual abuse is four times more common in girls, but the abuse of boys (or at least the reporting of such abuse) has increased significantly in the last decade.
- In nine out of ten cases, the child knows the abuser.
- In one out of ten cases, the father is the molester. Most abuse is committed by males. About 5 percent of the sexual abuse of girls and 20 percent of the sexual abuse of boys is committed by older females.
- Sexual abuse is usually a chronic situation. Child molesters don't recognize that they have a problem and don't seek help on their own.
- Sexual abuse often begins with something as innocent as sitting on an adult's lap or giving or receiving a back rub. Children often can't identify what is happening as the innocent gestures of affection progress into overt sexual abuse.
- Abuse usually proceeds over time from a situation in which an

adult has a child touch his genitals or he touches the child's genitals to situations involving oral-genital contact.

- Sexual abuse usually occurs clandestinely.
- In many cases, the child does not come forward to report the abuse because the abuser may be a trusted adult—a baby-sitter, teacher, or relative—whom the child does not want to get into trouble.
- Youngsters are often coerced into silence either through punishment or threats to themselves or to loved ones if they tell.

Spousal Abuse

The following is important information about spousal abuse that you should know.

- Children who live in families where there is spousal abuse are often as traumatized as the victim of the abuse. They are traumatized by the pain they see inflicted and by their feelings of powerlessness.
- Children who witness parental violence tend to model that behavior in their future intimate relationships.
- Women who are battered come from all economic and social classes.
- Although the use of alcohol is often implicated in the physical assaults, it is not unusual for the attacks to continue even when the batterer is no longer abusing alcohol.
- Most women who are abused try to leave the relationship. However, the abuser often prevents that from happening through coercion, physical threats, financial constraints, or confinement.
- My research has revealed a correlation between wife battering and child sexual abuse.

HOW CHILDREN REACT:
THE WARNING SIGNS OF ABUSE

Youngsters are unlikely to come forward and report that they are being abused. For some sexually abused children, in fact, what is happening may not seem bad. It may feel good. Why should they tell this to anyone?

Because youngsters are unlikely to tell you when they are being abused, how do you know when your suspicions are correct? One good tool is your intuition. If it's an idea that surfaces often but you keep pushing it out of your mind because it seems too unbelievable, trust your instincts enough to make inquiries.

Familiarize yourself with the following warning signs of sexual abuse. Remember that one isolated change in behavior is not cause for concern. However, a persistent pattern of the behavioral changes listed here should arouse your suspicion.

- *A sudden change in your child's feelings, awareness, or behavior in reference to sexuality.* This could be a teenager who becomes sexually promiscuous, or a preschooler who is suddenly masturbating excessively or is obsessed with sex to the point where that's all she talks about. It also might be a child knowing sexual information that is inappropriate for his age, like a seven-year-old boy who asks why white stuff comes out of a penis, or an eight-year-old girl who makes pictures of her family in which the father has a large erect penis.

  The opposite reactions may occur, too. Modesty can suddenly be taken to the extreme, such as a young child who hides in a closet to dress. A child may seem unable to tolerate any reference to sexuality at all. One of my patients was a thirteen-year-old girl who couldn't tolerate hearing or reading slang, four-letter curse words or, for that matter, any words about sex. To avoid these words, she learned to scan ahead and read without seeing the offending words.

- *Changes in a child's behavior.* In preschoolers, you may see increased clinging, a fear of specific adults, a loss of bowel or bladder control, or sleep disturbances. School-age children may have a sudden drop in school performance, social problems, or sleep disturbances. Adolescents may run away from home, attempt suicide, start to use drugs, or do things to injure themselves purposely.

- *Change in a child's normal emotional state.* In children of all ages, it's common to see fearfulness, worrying, anger, or depression that have no obvious relationship to what is going on in their lives. Sometimes, however, what you see is less rather than more emotion. In an attempt to hide the abuse, a child may withdraw and show no feelings.

Teenagers who have been sexually abused often express feelings of not fitting in with their peers. They say that they are different, strange, dirty, and evil. They say that they will never marry or have children. Some also talk intensely about feelings of mistrust and say they can never have faith in an adult. Others feel that they are always wrong and deserving of criticism from adults. Teens and adults who have been sexually abused as children tell me that they felt this way even as young children, but they didn't have the words then to express their feelings.

- *Physical problems.* Sexually abused children often develop a preoccupation with bodily concerns. They may complain of pain or itching in the genital areas or mouth. If they're young enough to require help bathing, they may become jumpy when you try to wash their genitalia. Eating disturbances are also common. Sexually abused children sometimes pull out their eyebrows, eyelashes, and head hair or may scar or mutilate their bodies.

MAKING YOUR CHILD FEEL SAFE

In cases of physical or sexual abuse, the following three steps should be considered.

1. *Call the authorities to report the incident.* Many precincts have specialized child abuse and child sexual abuse units to guide you through the complaint process. Let your child know that you've made a report. Do not say that the abuser will be thrown in jail for the rest of his or her life. That is more upsetting than reassuring to a child. Children want the abuse to stop, but they do not necessarily want the abuser to get into trouble. If the offender is threatened, the child may be reluctant to talk further about the abuse for fear of making the retribution even worse.

   After you've made your report, you can expect that the investigators and lawyers will need to talk to your child. Reduce the stress of this process by asking the authorities to limit the number of interviews with the child and to allow you to be present when the child is interviewed.

2. *Call the child's doctor to make an appointment.* The child should be examined for physical problems and sexually transmitted diseases. A clean bill of health is reassuring to you and to a child who is old enough to understand.

    If the abuse was of a serious nature or continued for an extended period of time, your child may need professional psychological counseling to recover. You also may want to seek help for yourself. Child abuse takes an emotional toll on both the child and the parent. If you do decide to get counseling, make sure that the mental health professional you see has experience in dealing with victims of abuse. Ask your pediatrician or the school guidance counselor for advice or a referral.

3. *Talk to the rest of the family about the abuse, both to inform them and to discover if another child had or is having a similar experience.* This may create some problems for the other children if they, too, had been abused but had not told. However, failing to discuss this matter with the other children creates a sense of secrecy that in my opinion has even greater negative consequences.

    I believe that the best way to inform the family is to make a calm, straightforward statement about what has happened without going into lurid details or becoming too emotional. You might say, "You're going to have a new baby-sitter. Annie told me that Mike made Annie touch his penis. Grown-ups should not ask a child to touch their private parts. This was wrong of him. I have called the police to let them know. I am sorry this happened to Annie, but I will do everything I can to make her and all of you feel safe."

DEBRIEFING FOR ABUSE

Now you can help your child begin to explore his or her feelings about what happened by using the four-step method of debriefing described in Chapter 4. Here are some suggestions for tailoring the debriefing to be most effective in situations of abuse. The following discussion focuses on sexual abuse, but this process can be used in all abuse situations.

Step I: Preparing Yourself

- *Learn what you can about what occurred.* Unlike other traumas, where you can do your own fact-finding without the child's help, abuse requires that you get most of your information about the incidents from the child. The abuser is not likely to be very cooperative. You won't be able to find out everything, but do find out whatever you can about what specifically occurred before talking with your child.

- *Be informed about sexual abuse.* Knowing the facts about sexual abuse is important so that you can ask the right questions to get the information you need, particularly if you're dealing with a case of suspected abuse. If you ask your seven-year-old daughter if Uncle Bob ever put his penis in her vagina and she says no, you might come away relieved, not knowing that he was having her perform oral sex, which is the more common form of sexual abuse in this age group.

  If you are knowledgeable, you will know how, where, and with whom sexual abuse can occur. Then you can prevent a reaction like, "Your brother? He would never do that! You're lying!" If you know about sexual abuse, you'd know that indeed the brother, the uncle, the father, or even the priest could do *that*.

- *Know the basics about children's sexual development.* Sexual abuse isn't always blatant. Almost every parent who has kissed a baby while diapering has wondered how low on the belly it is okay to kiss. Babies don't come with a red line that says, "Not below here," and a blue line that says, "Not above here." Often, in fact, abuse begins by subtly crossing the boundary of appropriateness for a given age. Two five-year-olds playing doctor is normal, but a twelve-year-old playing doctor with a five-year-old is not.

  Here is a brief synopsis of sexual development. If you need more detailed information on this subject, ask your pediatrician.

  - Infants (birth to age one). Sexuality in infants is defined by the pleasure they derive from sucking, being cuddled and rocked, clinging, and touching. Blankets, teddy bears, pacifiers, and thumbs are objects of desire.

- Preschoolers (ages two to five). The early years are called the anal stage because so much attention and tension is focused on controlling bladder and bowel. Lots of kissing and hugging goes on in this age group, and children become aware of and curious about the genital difference between boys and girls. This is the age when questions about where babies come from surface, as does bathroom humor—to the dismay of most parents. Some self-stimulation is common.
- School-age children (ages six to twelve). During the early part of this stage, children develop a sense of modesty, and their interest in and understanding about where babies come from increases. Some masturbation is common. It is not until the last couple of years that any evidence of puberty is noticeable. Even then, boys and girls stick mostly to same-sex groups. Gossip about who likes whom starts to surface, though, as does the telling of dirty jokes. Most children of this age will tell you, however, that the thought of kissing someone of the opposite sex is "gross."
- Teenagers (ages thirteen to eighteen). These are watershed years sexually. Girls start to menstruate, and boys begin to ejaculate. Interest in the opposite sex surges, and dating, kissing, petting, and sexual experimentation are commonplace, as is masturbation.
- *Practice talking about sex.*   Talking about sex with a child is uncomfortable for many adults, but in the case of sexual abuse, children will interpret that discomfort as a judgment against them. It's important to be at ease with the subject before talking to your child. You might want to practice talking with a friend or spouse or in front of a mirror. Use the proper words for the genitals so that you are comfortable when you sit down with your child. Make sure that you can identify body parts by name:
  - Female anatomy: breasts, nipples, vagina, clitoris, vulva
  - Male anatomy: penis, testicles
  - Human anatomy: anus, buttocks, urethra

Step II: Having the Child Tell the Story

In abuse, in contrast to other types of trauma, it is probable that as part of your preparation, you were able to gain from others only a few details about what actually occurred. To be most effective in helping your child, you will need to gain this information directly from the child. To gain the youngster's trust and cooperation so that he or she is more likely to be open and frank, the primary message you want to get across (regardless of what the abuser has said) is that the child is not to blame. Particularly in cases of physical abuse, children are often told that they brought the punishment on themselves by behaving badly. What you want the child to understand is that she does not deserve to be hurt.

In the case of sexual abuse, you must understand that the child was not a collaborator in the activity. Many adults initially respond to the suspicion or news of sexual abuse by blaming the child. They do this because their own sense of competence as a protective adult has been destroyed. Adults don't want to believe that their best efforts at caring for their children didn't protect them from harm. To preserve their self-image, it's easier to believe that the youngster did something to provoke the sexual encounter. Such reasoning restores the adult's sense of control over the child's well-being. However, this kind of thinking is not only faulty, but also harmful. Blaming the victims of sexual abuse compounds the emotional trauma they have already suffered. In reality, they did nothing to bring the abuse on themselves.

You might think of ways that you could have protected your youngster, but dwelling on them and making yourself sick with guilt won't help you or your child. Place the blame where it belongs— with the abuser.

The way that you should ask questions in the debriefing following abuse is different than in other traumas. Avoid asking leading questions because that might be used to benefit the abuser in any legal proceedings that ensue. You can encourage the child by saying, "What happened next?" or referring to something that the child has already offered and asking for an elaboration, such as, "You said that Uncle Harry's penis got big and hard. What happened after that?" What you should not do is ask if certain events happened. For example, do not ask, "Did Uncle Harry put his hand down your pants?"

Remember that children are often threatened with physical harm or other terrible repercussions for telling about abuse. It's important to reassure them that nothing will happen to them if they talk to you and that you will protect them from the abuser.

When the debriefing starts, your child may test the waters to see whether it really is safe to talk about what happened. How you listen and respond is important. Stay calm, even though you might hear things that anger, frighten, shame, surprise, or disgust you. Your reaction is crucial. If you respond by saying, "Why did you let Uncle Harry do that to you?" or "How could you let that happen without telling me?" your child will cut off communication. You might be expressing your concern and horror, but your child hears you blaming him for what happened. Remember that the abuser is always at fault; the child never is. By staying calm and reinforcing that the abuser has done a bad thing, you will encourage future communication and relieve the child of some guilt.

Don't be surprised if your child has large gaps in his memory of the abuse. Children who live in dire situations for long periods of time literally can't think about what is happening to them. They not only have to cope with experiencing this violation over and over, but also with the anticipation of the abuse. Think of the sexually abused daughter who lies wide-eyed in bed every night, waiting for the click of the door handle that alerts her to her father's presence. She knows that Daddy is going to do something terrible to her and it's just too awful to think about, so her mind goes blank.

If your child says that she can't remember what happened, don't press her for information. Just let her know that you are always ready to listen if she does recall more.

When young children tell the story, dolls may be particularly helpful. I recommend against the use of anatomically correct dolls, which many children find frightening. Often, the genitalia are more detailed than the faces. To my mind, these dolls encourage children to make up things because of their grotesquely exaggerated genitalia. There's very little a child can't show with two rag dolls.

Older children may want to do this part of the debriefing while taking a walk so that they don't have to look you in the eye while they describe the embarrassing details of their experience.

It may be hard for you to believe what your child has to say, but you'd be doing any child a disservice by chalking up a story of sexual abuse to an overactive imagination. Children generally don't make up stories of abuse. Trust your child. Keeping these thoughts in mind, listen to your child to find out what happened.

Step III: Sharing the Child's Reaction

The third step of this debriefing provides an opportunity for you to reassure the child and correct any misconceptions. For instance, I once saw a sexually abused boy who told me that he believed that the children in school thought he was ugly. Before the abuse, the child had never expressed such feelings. I talked to his mother about his feelings, and she said that her son had many friends in school and that the children did not think him ugly.

I worked with the mother and gave her some ideas about how she could help her son. She told him that sometimes when bad things happen to a little boy, he feels ugly, but he isn't ugly outside or inside. She told him that she loved him and that the feeling he had of being ugly would go away. It would just take time.

Step IV: Survival and Recovery

In this step, the debriefer helps the child make a plan to feel safer and to protect herself from future abuse. You should focus on helping the child find ways to feel better about herself and to restore her faith in others. Here are some things you can do to help your child:

* *Find a support group for your child made up of other children who have had similar experiences.*   Ask your school counselor for advice.
* *Help your child reestablish the sense of self-respect and privacy that has been violated.*   Start by telling your child that he is special and should always be treated in a caring, respectful way, not only by you, but by all of the people in his life. Explain that part of showing respect is recognizing his right to privacy. His body is his own, and no one should ask to see or touch it in a way that makes him uncomfortable.

    Try to find areas in the home for your child where no one can go without his permission. Make a point of knocking on his door when you enter his room, and ask permission before taking anything of his or reorganizing his belongings. Showing your child that you respect his right to privacy will drive home your verbal message that he is entitled to that right wherever he is and that no one—not even another adult—has the right to violate it.

    Tell your child that one of the ways you treat him like a special person is by taking care of his body and teaching him how to take care of himself. That's why you make sure he brushes his teeth, takes a bath, and wears a seatbelt in the car. You want to protect him from physical harm, and you expect the other people in his life to do the same. Make the point that no one has the right to hurt him, regardless of his behavior, and that he should always let you know if someone threatens him.

- *Help the child make a distinction between secrets that should be kept and those that should be told to a trusted adult.*   You might say, for instance, "A secret to keep would be what you bought a friend for her birthday. However, if someone asks you to keep a secret about an activity that makes you uncomfortable or that hurts you, you should always tell me or another adult, like your teacher."
- *Let the youngster know that you want to be her confidant.*   Tell your child that you value her opinion and want to hear about her feelings, whether it's something as ordinary as what she wants packed in her lunch, or something as disturbing as where her neighbor touched her when she went to sell him wrapping paper for a school fund drive.

Even though abuse is an uncomfortable subject that you will probably want to deal with and put behind you, don't be in a hurry to shut the door on communication about this subject. Most children may need to go through some parts of the debriefing more than once to grapple with what happened to them. If the abuse lasted a long time, it may take several months or even years for your child to overcome the fears and anxieties that make nighttime scary or concentrating on schoolwork difficult. Professional counseling may help speed the recovery, but—with or without counseling—your patience, understanding, and willingness to listen are an invaluable part of the process.

7

NATURAL DISASTERS
Shared Devastation

U nlike other traumas, which mostly affect one person or one family or at most a few families, natural disasters usually traumatize whole communities. The physical disruption caused by a natural disaster may last for months or even years. Natural disasters can leave people without jobs, homes, and schools. Some people even lose their community completely. A year after the floods in the Midwest, for instance, the government decided to move a whole town off the floodplain rather than raise the plain itself. These people relived the trauma of the flood as they again lost their homes and familiar surroundings.

WHAT YOU SHOULD KNOW ABOUT NATURAL DISASTERS

Why are natural disasters so unsettling? Most survivors mention the following:

- *Lost sense of security.* Natural disasters are unexpected. Even if a hurricane or flood is predicted, the intensity of the natural occurrence cannot be accurately determined ahead of time. People cannot fully prepare themselves for these events. There are constant physical reminders of the disaster as the community tries to recover. Buildings remained boarded up following Hurricane Andrew in Florida, and yellow and red tape surrounded some buildings in Los Angeles long after the Northridge earthquake.

Survivors often worry about the next disaster. Will it come next week or next year? The uncertainty haunts survivors.

- *Loss of familiar surroundings.*　Natural disasters take away familiar landmarks. We feel lost when the fast-food restaurant on the corner or the big tree in front of our neighbor's house is gone. Landmarks orient us in our community and give us the comforting feeling of being home. I had an experience, for instance, of trying to find my way to a community hospital in Florida following Hurricane Andrew. When I called for directions, the nurse said, "Make a left at the chicken place. Wait, that's not there anymore. Okay, make a left at the . . . nope, no street signs either. Oh, yes. Make a left where the army has stored a pile of donated clothes." She couldn't think of a landmark that hadn't been destroyed by the storm. To the people living in that community, it no longer looked like home because the hurricane had removed all of the familiar signposts that were the environmental touchstones of their daily lives.

- *Loss of personal possessions.*　Natural disasters can result in a loss of most or all of our personal possessions. Much of what is lost is irreplaceable: heirlooms, mementos, photos, those special things that gave comfort. I remember a story told by a soldier who hadn't been at home when Hurricane Andrew hit South Florida. After the storm, he was having difficulty finding his house because the whole neighborhood had been decimated. About two blocks from his house he suddenly stopped the car and got out. There in the road was a stuffed toy that had been his since he was a little boy. Seeing his toy abandoned in the road brought home to this tough soldier all the losses he had suffered in the hurricane, and he sat down on the curb and cried.

HOW CHILDREN REACT TO NATURAL DISASTERS

Although most youngsters don't develop emotional illness following a natural disaster, most show some distressed behavior temporarily, such as clinging, regression in developmental skills, and repetitive play that reflects their experience of the disaster. The scope of such behavioral changes depends on the extent and severity of the trauma:

Were there high winds only, or was the whole house blown away? Did the house just shake, or did the family have to flee from home because the walls began to fall? Did you suffer just minor scrapes and bumps, or did you lose a family member? Are the fires still burning? Are you back in your home or apartment? Are reminders still there, or has your community returned to some semblance of normalcy? Was this the only trauma in your child's recent life, or did it follow a string of stresses, such as the death of a pet or a divorce? Finally, were the adults in your child's life calm and stable, or were they distraught and overwhelmed? Children can't figure out for themselves how much danger they're in, so they often rely on the reactions of the adults closest to them as a barometer of how secure—or insecure—they are.

Children feel their losses following a natural disaster as keenly as adults do. However, what disturbs a child is often quite different from what concerns adults. It's important to know what kinds of things are important to children so that you don't dismiss genuine feelings of fear or loss over something that may seem trivial to you. A small child might be concerned about a missing blanket and not at all concerned about where the next meal is coming from. Children of different ages have different reactions to natural disasters.

Preschoolers (Ages Two to Five)

Very young children don't know how to handle the anxiety they feel following a natural disaster. They don't have the vocabulary to express their fears, nor do they have the competence to understand what actually happened. Play is one of the few tools that young children have to express their feelings. After a disaster, little ones may play the same scene over and over. They will use whatever they have to represent the destructive force of nature they witnessed. In the aftermath of the Northridge earthquake, for example, the preschool kids I debriefed built great towers of blocks on the table and then gave the table a powerful shake to knock over the blocks. Again and again, the children repeated the game. After a hurricane, broccoli on the dinner plate can stand in for the trees that were blown down in the storm.

Preschool children also personify storms. Very young children who survived Hurricane Andrew called it One-Eyed Andrew. One-Eyed Andrew was a monster. He was mean. He was fast, and he was strong. He came at night, took away their toys, and then, according to the television reporters, he died. Afterward, the preschoolers worried that another monster might come along. They remained clingy and afraid to be alone in their rooms, especially at night.

School-Age Children (Ages Six to Twelve)

In contrast to preschoolers, school-age children can take in the destruction to the larger community rather than focus only on themselves. Thus, they are particularly frightened about separation. They worry about what would happen if they are at school or somewhere else when a natural disaster strikes and they cannot get to their families. Kids in this age group are more likely to understand news reports detailing the number of people who died during a natural disaster. Thus they fear that they or their parents might die if the storm, earthquake, or fire strikes again. As a result, school-age children, like their younger counterparts, often show anxiety around separation, whether going to school or going to bed at night, even when such everyday good-byes had been routine for years.

School-age children are more aware of the vulnerabilities of their parents. They often lose their absolute faith in their parents' ability to protect them since their parents were not able to avert the effects of the disaster. They may also lose their trust in the adult community's wisdom as a whole. John, a ten-year-old who survived Hurricane Andrew, mused acerbically that the emergency crew evacuated Grandma from her home in Miami Beach to his home. For reasons beyond his ability to understand, they didn't move his family from their home, yet it was their house with Grandma in it that came crashing down around them. Now they were all living in Grandma's house, which the storm had hardly touched.

Loss of personal belongings is particularly difficult for school-age youngsters, who create large and intricate collections of dolls, cards, baseball caps, action figures, and the like. These boys and girls spend much of their time alone playing with or simply taking inventory of their collections. They also use them as a way to make friends and socialize. When looked at in this light, it's not hard to understand why losing what looks like a pile of junk to an adult is terribly upsetting to a child in this age group.

Whereas preschoolers turn natural disasters into monsters, school-age children are more likely to have fantasies about the forces behind them. For instance, children in the California communities affected by the Northridge earthquake were taught about the causes of the quake. They learned about the plates of the earth. Their teachers demonstrated how the plates pushed up against each other by using their hands overlapping each other at an angle. When I later debriefed the children and asked what they knew about the cause of the earthquake, they solemnly told me about the plates in the earth. They mimicked what their teacher did with her hands. Then I said, "That's what your teacher told you, but what do you think happened?" "King Kong came. He stomped on everything," they answered in unison.

Teenagers (Ages Thirteen to Eighteen)

Natural disasters are particularly disruptive to teens. If the disaster results in school closing, temporary or permanent relocation, or loss of telephone service, teens lose their primary social connection—their friends. Unlike younger children, who still rely on their parents for their comfort and security, teenagers have begun to shift that role to their peers. They are often more comfortable sharing feelings of vulnerability and fear with their friends than with their parents.

Teens also need their privacy more than younger kids. It's not just a luxury at this age, but a developmental necessity. If a natural disaster has uprooted a family and sent it to a shelter or to a relative's home, teenagers may lose the sanctuary of their own space, whether it's a room of their own or just a corner they've claimed as theirs somewhere in the house.

Finally, because natural disasters often have a catastrophic effect on local businesses, teens often lose their after-school jobs, which provide the spending money that gives them some independence from their parents.

Under normal circumstances, teenagers have a hard time balancing the conflicting needs of being both a dependent child and an emerging adult. In the aftermath of a trauma, their conflicting feelings are greatly magnified. The tug of adult responsibility makes them more aware of what they should do—and often of their failure in a crisis to be all they want to be. For instance, sixteen-year-old Mark remembered being told that the safest place to be in the house during an earthquake was under a sturdy door frame. So when the earth shook in the middle of the night, he leapt out of bed and ran under the doorjamb. When the quake was over, he realized that in his panic he had left his little brother in bed, exposed to harm. Mark was so burdened with guilt that he wouldn't let his brother out of his sight for weeks following the earthquake.

Teenagers themselves have identified the coping mechanisms they feel are most successful in helping them get through a crisis. They are, in order of importance, talking to friends, listening to music, watching television, crying, and going to the movies. Unfortunately, many of these options aren't available after a natural disaster, so teens are left alone to handle their feelings of loss and vulnerability.

Teenagers often see their situation in the extreme. They tend to think that they will never see their friends again, will never have a normal life again, will never be able to get back to school and continue with their life. Some act out their feelings of helplessness by fighting, using drugs or alcohol, overeating, or other excessive behavior.

DEBRIEFING FOR NATURAL DISASTERS

On television you often hear commentators, both professional and lay, say you should hug your children and reassure them; but you say, "How can I reassure them when I don't know that everything will turn out all right?" You can't. What you can do, however, is encourage them to tell you what they saw, what they felt, what they experienced that was disturbing, and what they worry about. As mentioned in Chapter 4, debriefing is a structured four-step method that will allow you to offer support to children after a trauma. You'll find the general instructions about how to conduct a debriefing in that chapter. Take the time, also, to review Chapter 3 to become familiar with the posttraumatic reactions that are normal for children of different ages. There are several ways to tailor a debriefing to focus on the unique experience of living through a natural disaster.

Step I: Preparing Yourself

Children feel reassured when they have an opportunity to express their feelings to someone who will listen. The last part of that statement is key. If you are too overwhelmed with other considerations to sit and listen to your child, you can't help much.

Determine how emotionally able you are to offer support. To do this, review the seven natural disaster trauma-related stresses below to find out how greatly you were affected:

1. Was the natural disaster actually life threatening to you, or did you believe that it was?
2. Did the death of a person or pet occur?
3. How much damage did your home sustain? Can you still live in the house, or was the destruction so great that major reconstruction is necessary to make it safe again?
4. How much money will you be getting to help you rebuild? Will the funds from insurance and the Federal Emergency Management Agency (FEMA) be enough, or will you be in serious financial trouble?
5. Did the disaster lead to a loss of income due to the disruption or loss of a job or child care?
6. How safe do you feel now?
7. How prepared were you? People who were prepared for the disaster feel much better than those who weren't—even if their houses fell down. Those who weren't prepared often feel guilty, believing that they could have done something to help themselves and their families and they didn't.

Adults whose lives have been so disrupted that they need to spend all of their time handling emergency measures to get food, clothing, and shelter for the family might want to consider getting help with the debriefing. You might be better off calling on a close friend or relative who wasn't affected by the natural disaster to debrief the children rather than trying to provide the emotional support yourself.

Step II: Having the Child Tell the Story

Direct your questions to the unusual sights, sounds, and smells that often accompany a natural disaster. You might ask your child the following:

*   *What kinds of smells do you remember?*   Pungent, scary smells often accompany natural disasters. There is often the smell of natural gas from ruptured gas lines, the smell of smoke and fire,

or the smell of spoiled food left in the kitchen when the electricity was no longer working.

- *What kinds of sounds do you remember?*   Natural disasters are accompanied by frightening sounds: the wind howling, windows blowing out, walls falling down, glass breaking. Small children locked in a room for safety don't know what is causing the sounds. They can only imagine the terrible things that are waiting to get to them just beyond the door.

- *What do you remember seeing?*   The world turns topsy-turvy during natural disasters. Tall trees fall over like sticks. Houses that are supposed to provide security against the elements are blown apart piece by piece.

- *What do you think caused the natural disaster?*   When your child gives you his account of the disaster, you'll see how he processes the event through his own perspective on the world. Young children, in particular, may end up with a distorted view of the cause of a natural disaster as they try to make sense out of information they get from television reports and from overheard adult conversations. Thus, they might attribute an earthquake to King Kong or a hurricane to aliens landing on earth. It's important to know what misconceptions your child has about the cause of a natural disaster so that you can give him a more accurate explanation.

Step III: Sharing the Child's Reaction

- *Let your child know that you take her concerns seriously, no matter how minor they may appear to you.*   Older children, in particular, may feel guilty for being upset about their personal losses, which seem minor when compared to the devastation they see all around them. They may be reluctant to bring them up, fearing that you'll think them petty and self-absorbed.

  Lisa and Ann, two teenage sisters who survived Hurricane Andrew, felt this way. They had just moved into a house, and finally, after sharing a room all of their lives, each had her own room. The bedrooms they had so carefully fixed up were now dirty and water-damaged. Lisa and Ann felt as if part of the pleasure of enjoying their new rooms had been taken from them, but they were afraid to tell their parents. They thought they would be ridiculed for being upset about the minor damage to their belongings when so many others in the community had lost everything.

It was important for Lisa and Ann to know that their disappointment was understandable, appropriate, and deserved sympathy. You should do the same for the small losses of your child. Do not tell her how lucky she was not to have suffered greater misfortune like others around her.

- *Help your child recognize the losses that others have suffered, as well.* It's important to validate your child's losses, but it's also good to let him know that others have suffered, as well. Children then not only feel badly about what they have lost, but can sympathize with their friends, who have lost important things, too. Letting kids know that others suffered losses also helps them understand that they weren't singled out for punishment.

- *Help a dislocated child living in a shelter or a relative's house recognize that the situation is temporary.* Children wonder if they will ever have a home or a room with their own toys or their own telephone again. Let them know that this temporary living condition will not go on forever. They *will* have a home to live in again.

- *Tell a child who is still experiencing anxiety caused by the disaster that those feelings will lessen over time.* Your child will eventually sleep better. He or she won't always be afraid of buildings crashing down. It just takes time.

Step IV: Survival and Recovery

The following have been found to work particularly well in the aftermath of a natural disaster.

- *Give a gift of a stuffed toy.* In public, older children may roll their eyes at the offer of a teddy bear, but at night in makeshift lodgings it's another story. You'll probably find even a brusque teenage boy curled up around a new stuffed toy for the comfort it provides.

- *Conduct preparedness drills.* Develop a plan with your child about what your family will do in the event of another natural disaster. The complexity of the plan will depend, of course, on the age of the child. However, even young children can learn to keep shoes under the bed, learn to get to the doorjamb for safety, or know in which room the family should gather in the event of another storm. This is not intended to be an inclusive list of how to prepare for natural disasters. Your local Red Cross and other community agencies can give you more complete details on what preparations are most suitable in your community.

- *Make an emergency plan.* Because being prepared gives a sense of security, involve your child in making plans so that everybody will be ready in the event of another natural disaster. Have the youngster help you find a place in each room to store a flashlight and make a schedule for checking the batteries. Shop for water and food supplies that will be stashed for an emergency. Choose a relative outside of the area who will be the family contact in the event of a natural disaster, and explain to older children how to call collect so they know they can reach the relative even if they don't have any money. Explain what steps will be taken to reunite the family if a disaster should strike when you are at work or the children are at school.
- *Teach relaxation skills.* Work with your child to develop a relaxation routine, whether it's deep breathing, counting from a hundred or ten down to one, or imagining some favorite peaceful place.

All of these efforts will give your child a sense of control that counteracts the most frightening part of these traumas for children—the loss of their sense of security.

8

DIVORCE

When Parents Cause the Pain

Divorce is almost unremarkable today, with almost one out of every two marriages breaking up. Even so, none of us is inured to the pain and confusion that we feel when our family is broken apart, particularly not our children.

For years, the two of you have protected your children, and now you are taking their world apart. What can you and your mate do when you no longer wish to be together but you are both concerned about the children? For one thing, you can gain an understanding about how your divorce will affect your children. Then you can use the debriefing method described in Chapter 4 in conjunction with the information in this chapter to help your children cope with the inevitable changes in their lives that come with divorce.

WHAT YOU SHOULD KNOW
ABOUT DIVORCE

In the last decade, more than half of the married couples seeking a divorce had children. The prevailing attitude toward divorce was that if it was good for the parents, it must also be good for the children. Particularly because it had became so common, divorce wasn't thought to be traumatic for children.

During the eighties, however, researchers began to collect information from ongoing studies that looked at the long-term effects of divorce on families. The latest results of those studies, which have become available only recently, show that our assumptions about the effects of divorce on children were inaccurate. Divorce is not a normal experience just because many people go through it. To children, it is a life-changing, traumatic event. They are the powerless victims in the divorce. They have no say in the decision, they are pushed around psychologically, and in some cases they are even used as pawns by irresponsible parents. Each and every child who goes through a divorce wonders, "Why me?"

For most children, the effects of divorce in the early years following the separation are transitory, albeit difficult. It is in the teenage and young adult years that the long-range effects become apparent, and they appear to be intense and long lasting. Here are some of the results of the studies:

- Half of the children grew up subjected to the anger and hostility that their parents continued to harbor for each other even after the divorce.
- Three in five children felt rejected by at least one parent, often by the noncustodial parent who dropped out of the child's life.
- One in four children experienced a large drop in their standard of living.
- One-half of the children went through a second divorce within ten years.
- In the preschool and early school-age years, boys had a harder time than girls in adjusting emotionally to divorce. Their performance in school suffered and they had trouble handling aggression with friends.
- Over time, however, the boys' behavior tended to improve while the girls' behavior tended to become more upset and emotional.
- Over half of the children grew up to be worried, underachieving, self-deprecating, and sometimes angry adolescents and young adults.
- The most critical long-term effect was the development of significant relationship problems. Children of divorce were likely to be afraid to trust relationships and hesitant about making a commitment to a specific person.

THE THREE STAGES OF DIVORCE

What this research makes clear is that the negative effects of divorce, which were once thought to be short-lived, are in fact long lasting. A divorce is an ongoing process that has three stages: the crisis stage, the short-term stage, and the long-term stage.

The time frames given here for these three stages of divorce are approximate. Your child's experience may be quite different, depending on the circumstances of your divorce.

Stage 1: The Crisis Stage

Divorce actually begins with the couple's decision to separate. This is the event that precipitates the crisis stage. The crisis stage can begin when the parents tell the child about their decision, or it can begin when one parent leaves suddenly and files for divorce. The child wakes up one morning and finds the parent gone. During the crisis stage, the child's world is shattered. He loses one parent. He loses his normal home life. He loses his sense of stability.

This is a time of shock and disbelief for almost all children. Regardless of how much conflict between the parents preceded the divorce, children just assume that life is like that in marriage, and they assume that their parents will stay together. The only time that children may wish for divorce is in extreme cases of battering or alcoholism, where life is so horrible that children see divorce as an escape from their domestic hell.

In the crisis stage, the following stressors have the greatest effect on children:

- *Parental conflict* is the single most serious stressor during the crisis stage. The conflict comes with the territory. The sensitivity that most parents usually have toward a child's concerns disappears when they become enmeshed in a conflict with their partner about a separation. Where they might have tried to maintain some control over their anger when they were still trying to save their marriage, now they can pull out all the stops because their vows have been broken. Parents not only say bad things to and about each other within the child's earshot, but they even resort to pushing and shoving each other.

Obviously, bitter displays of anger and resentment should be kept away from children. However, a divorcing couple also shouldn't strive to be too friendly because this confuses the children. After all, if you can get along so well, why can't you stay married? Also, a too-friendly relationship fuels a child's reconciliation fantasies. Thus a moderate amount of conflict between a divorcing couple makes the breakup understandable to kids without making them suffer the trauma of seeing an outwardly violent or bitterly contentious relationship between their parents.

- *The depressed state* in which children see their parents is another stressor. It's not unusual for both parents to be depressed and cry, regardless of whether they want the divorce. Both the departing spouse and the remaining spouse suffer a loss, and it upsets kids to see this.

- *Financial distress* is another stressor during divorce, especially for women. Wives usually lose a significant portion of their household income while becoming the custodial parent 90 percent of the time.

- *Loss of attention and concern* from parents is also disruptive to children. A father who is no longer living with the children probably doesn't have regular visitation scheduled yet and is not a reliable emotional support. At the same time, the custodial parent—more often than not the mother—is anxious and depressed and has less emotional reserves to deal with her children, so she may be impatient and yell more often. The mother may have to return to work or work longer at her job to earn money or as a way of avoiding her grief over the loss of the marriage. When she's not working, she's likely to be socializing more, again as a way to forget her sorrow.

- *Loss of the father* is the final stressor in the crisis stage of a divorce, because 90 percent of custodial parents are mothers. Of the noncustodial parents, most have less than biweekly contact with their children, and even that decreases over time. For children, then, divorce often means the partial or complete loss of the father.

The resolution of this crisis stage comes when one parent decides to move out, the other parent finds a place to live, and a new order of life is established. The child is in day care or after-school programs now because the mother has to work. Mom has regular nights out with her friends. Dad comes to pick up the kids every other weekend.

Stage 2: The Short-Term Stage

This stage lasts approximately one to two years following the immediate crisis. The stressors children experience most often during this stage include the following:

- *The recognition that this is what life will be from now on.* That recognition is shocking: Mom and Dad don't live together. Our family will never be together again.
- *Parental hostility often continues.* Particularly in couples who are still separated and haven't divorced yet, children often hear hostility from both sides. The mother might say, "Is your father still seeing that home wrecker he was dating?" The father might chime in with, "Is your mother still keeping such a dirty house?"
- *Older children are often drafted as an ally for one parent or another.* The parent, feeling lonely, turns to an older child for comfort. It's not unusual to see children, even teenagers, sleeping with the parent. Most parents will make an excuse for this arrangement, but it is usually the parent's choice.

    Relying on children for company and comfort isn't healthy for kids. One of the developmental tasks for children is learning to go to bed by themselves. In younger children who haven't achieved this independence, sleeping with the parent inhibits them from accomplishing this task. When older children—who have already learned to say good night and stay in their own bed—are asked to sleep with the parent, they suffer a setback.
- *The custodial parent often pushes the child to take on adult responsibilities at home.* Because the custodial parent is stressed, the child may be pressed to take on more chores. To a certain extent, this doesn't cause a problem. However, if youngsters take on too much—all of the cooking, cleaning, and baby-sitting, for instance—it can be detrimental. They often end up giving up their peer relationships and developing independence.

- *Parents often begin dating.* Parental dating heightens the child's awareness of his or her parents' sexuality. In a marriage, the parents have a sexual relationship, but it is not so overt around the children that they take note of it. However, when a mother dresses up in sexy clothes or brings home a man who is physically affectionate with her in front of the children—even with nothing more than hugs and kisses—children, especially older children, can't ignore the sexual inferences of the behavior.

Stage 3: The Long-Term Stage

Usually, this stage begins somewhere at the end of the first or second year after the crisis stage.

- *The parental hostility sometimes continues.* The children are used as messengers. "Tell your daddy that the support check didn't get here on time," Mom says. "Tell your mom to stop being such a nag," says Dad. When this happens, children feel torn because of their loyalty to both parents.
- *One parent can't let go of the relationship and is still in mourning.* This parent, hoping the couple can reconcile, is stuck emotionally in the crisis stage and, because of his or her own distress, can't offer the children the emotional support they need.
- *The mother and the children may become enmeshed in a relationship* that is too close. Without the husband to divert some of her attention and affection, the mother now focuses all of her emotional attachment on the children. This attachment can make the necessary developmental task of breaking away from home difficult.
- *Parents may remarry during this stage.* The introduction of a new relationship has some effects on the way the parents relate to their children. There is a decrease in the attention of the custodial parent toward the children as attention is now shared with the new spouse. Consequently, the children often feel a loss of the custodial parent.
- *Remarriage also brings with it the loss of the child's fantasy of reconciliation.* Children may feel distressed by their feelings

of disloyalty toward the noncustodial parent. They feel that if they like the new spouse, it is a sign of disloyalty to the parent.

Unless they are very young, children usually also resent the new stepparent's attempts to assign chores or dole out discipline. (Smart stepparents, in fact, won't even try these things initially but will defer to the biological parent.)

- *Finally, if there is no remarriage, the family will usually live on a much lower income.* As a result, children have to go without many of the things that they were used to having before the divorce.

HOW CHILDREN REACT TO DIVORCE

A child's reaction to divorce is shaped by three variables: age, gender, and the stage of divorce. Children of different ages think and act differently. A five-year-old girl in the crisis stage of divorce will have different emotional reactions from a twelve-year-old boy in the crisis stage of divorce.

To understand what your child is experiencing, it is important to consider all three of these variables. The discussion in this chapter is divided in segments according to the child's age: preschoolers, school-age children, and teenagers. Each age group is then divided by stage of divorce: crisis, short-term, and long-term. All children age, and all divorces go through each stage. Accordingly, you will want to refer to this chapter as your child ages or as the stage of the divorce progresses from crisis to short-term to long-term.

To use this chapter, you will need to look up the appropriate age group for your child and read the introduction following the age heading. This will give you an overview of your child's cognitive and emotional levels as they relate to a divorce. Then find the segment that addresses the stage of divorce you are in, which will give you more detail of the likely responses or reactions that your child is experiencing at this time and what you can do to assist him or her. I believe that you may find it helpful to review the other segments, both age and stage of divorce, too. It will give you a better appreciation for what your child has been through and for the different issues that may lie ahead.

Preschoolers (Ages Two to Five)

What does the preschooler bring to the divorce situation? For one thing, children in this age group see themselves at the center of everything. When something happens in the world around them, preschoolers believe that they are the cause of it. In the case of divorce, they will feel that they are somehow responsible for the parents' breaking up. When you tell a preschooler that you're getting a divorce, the child commonly asks, "Why? Because I was bad?"

Children in this age group also have difficulty separating what is real from what is imagined. A child's fantasy can become so compelling that he or she acts as if it is about to happen. In the case of divorce, preschoolers may develop a fantasy about being abandoned by their mother just as they were by their father and may become terribly distressed and fearful every time the mother goes out.

Though preschoolers spend a lot of time in fantasy, they nonetheless are mature enough to have a rudimentary understanding of some abstract ideas. For instance, preschoolers understand the purpose of money. When they hear that there are money problems, they may interpret that to mean that there isn't enough money, which is an accurate appraisal. However, they may not be mature enough to understand what that really means to them, and they often imagine an extreme scenario that has nothing to do with reality. Preschoolers may become convinced, for instance, that they're going to starve to death for lack of grocery money, or that they're going to end up living on the street because there won't be enough money for a home. It's important, therefore, to be as concrete as possible when describing to a preschooler how life is going to change after a divorce.

Crisis Stage

In a divorce, the preschooler's temperament shapes her reaction. Divorce means a lot of change. There may be a new day-care arrangement and a new home. Dad might suddenly not be there anymore, and Mom might not be as attentive as she used to be. All of these changes will be hardest on the preschooler who adapts poorly to change. That child will balk more than a more complacent counterpart. Divorcing parents, who have little reserves of patience given the stress on them, might find it easier to be sympathetic to a recalcitrant three-year-old if they keep in mind that the child isn't being difficult to make life harder for them. The child is simply overwhelmed by all of the new routines that are being introduced. As time goes on and the preschooler adapts to her new routines, she'll be easier to live with.

When considering how preschoolers experience the crisis stage of divorce, parents should also keep in mind that this is the age during which children intensify their attachment to the father. Up until now, they have focused mostly on the mother for comfort, feeding, and playing. As preschoolers become more independent, they begin to include people other than the primary caregiver in their lives, and they get closer to the father. Divorce, in most instances, removes the father and interrupts the development of this new closeness.

Short-Term Stage

If your child is a preschooler during the short-term stage of your divorce, he or she was a toddler when you first divorced. Even though some time has passed and a new life has begun, some problems of the crisis stage linger in the short-term stage. Even after the initial separation, for instance, parents often continue to fight over child support and visitation. Preschoolers experience even a brief flare-up as a big fight. Add that perspective to a vivid imagination, and you can see how a preschooler could witness parents having a big fight and think, "Oh, my God. Mommy and Daddy are going to kill each other." Obviously, parents would do well to keep bitter arguments out of the earshot of children of this age.

The continued disruption of routines also affects preschoolers in the short-term stage. Perhaps the mother had a maintenance agreement whereby she was given some support for the first year after the separation and now she has to find a job and send the child to day care full-time. Perhaps the custodial parent, after trying to hold on to the family home, has decided that it is not economically feasible, and she's selling it and moving to a new apartment. Obviously, the continued change in routine only serves to keep children feeling insecure and on edge.

The emotional distress of the custodial parent also affects children of this age. Little children often reflect their parents' moods. When the parents are up, they're up, too. When the parents are down, these little ones are down, too.

Preschoolers who go through a divorce depend almost entirely on their custodial parent—most often the mother—for their emotional support. Unlike older children, they don't have peer relationships to support them. During this period, the custodial parent may still be distraught on the one hand and actively seeking to develop a new social life that excludes the children on the other. Young children often feel, rightfully, that the parent is not as available to them emotionally as she was before the divorce. She's less patient and more dismissive and doesn't seem to want to spend as much time with them as she used to. All of this makes preschoolers feel that they are losing touch with the mother at the same time that they are feeling abandoned by the father, too.

They are, by and large, abandoned by the father, who might visit often for a few months, but then move on to another relationship. The father might skip one visitation and then another, until in some cases he doesn't come at all. That absence affects preschool girls and boys differently. For boys, the loss of the father also means the loss of a role model. At this age, boys begin to emulate their fathers. Preschool boys try to walk and talk like their dads. Without this strong masculine presence, boys have no one to emulate. Given this reality, the custodial parent would do well by the child to bring another male role model into his life, such as an uncle or a grandfather. Obviously, this person can't replace the father, but he can at least partially fill the void left by the father's absence.

For preschool girls, the father is the person who helps confirm the value of their femaleness. Dads make their little girls feel that it's nice and good to be a girl, that girls are nice to have around. As the father becomes less available in the short-term stage of divorce, there's less chance for girls to get this message.

At the same time, the absence of the father makes it more likely that young girls will develop a relationship that is too close with the mother. The father isn't there to share the daughter's affection and allegiance, and the mother-daughter bond often becomes so intense that it has to break apart violently during adolescence because it is too close a connection to naturally loosen as the girl grows older.

For children in this age group, joint custody, which would keep the connection with the father strong, is difficult to handle. It is very difficult for preschoolers to go between two households because their cognitive and memory capabilities do not allow them to understand the connection and the difference between the two households. They are where they are, and the other place might as well not exist. Even if the other house is only four blocks away, it might as well be at the end of the world for younger children because they can't remember it when they are not there. Also, younger children find it very difficult being away from their primary parent—usually the mother—for any length of time.

Long-Term Stage

If you are now in the long-term stage of your divorce, one or two years have passed since your separation. Your preschooler was just an infant when you made the decision to get divorced and probably has no memory of living in an intact family. Many parents believe that in this situation, children probably think of the divorced family as the norm, never having known any other situation. However, research tells us that this is not the case. Divorce still marks the child's development.

If, as often happens, the father has long been absent, preschoolers don't miss that person per se. Rather, they suffer from the chronic absence of a father. They live in a house where there never was a daddy or where there was only a picture of a daddy to fill the void. Preschoolers, who read books about families and see other children with both parents, feel like "the kid without a daddy." As one child said, "All boys and girls have a daddy, but I don't."

The long-term absence of a father makes preschoolers more receptive to a stepparent who is most likely to come into their lives during this stage of divorce. Preschoolers who have lost touch with their fathers have no memory of that relationship at all, so they don't feel that they are betraying anyone by accepting a stepfather into their lives. Even the preschoolers who do have an ongoing relationship with their dads accept a stepfather readily. They may know their father, but they don't remember him as part of the family unit, so they're more receptive to a stepparent.

While preschoolers are more accepting of their custodial parent's new partner, they may also have conflicting feelings of jealousy about losing the custodial parent's total attention. Preschoolers who are in the long-term stage of divorce are accustomed to Mom being the only grown-up at home and to having her complete and undivided attention. When a new father comes to live with the family, the children have to share not only Mom's attention, but her affection as well, and that can breed feelings of jealousy and anger toward the new parent.

Signs of Distress

Preschoolers, by their very nature, can be a cantankerous lot. They can shriek, "I hate you!" just because you make them turn off the video they've watched four times already. How do you know when a preschooler's emotional instability is normal and when it is a sign of distress over changes in home life? You can look for the following signs as indications of emotional distress:

- *Loss of developmental accomplishments.* If a child had stopped sucking his thumb but starts again, or if he had been completely dry at night but suddenly begins having a rash of bed-wetting, these "regressions" might be indications of emotional distress.
- *Failure to acquire new developmental skills.* Developmental skills are acquired by fits and starts according to the child's in-born script, so there's usually no need to worry if your youngster isn't keeping up with her peers. However, if you notice that the child has stalled developmentally for an unusually long period, it may be a sign that psychological distress is thwarting the child's personal growth.
- *Emotional inconsistency.* Preschoolers can be moody, but their moods are usually predictable. You know which events provoke which emotional states. When a preschooler is emotionally un-predictable and inconsistent, it may be that the stresses in his life are overwhelming him.
- *Anger toward playmates that wasn't there before.* If a child is suddenly argumentative with youngsters with whom she had always played harmoniously, it may be a sign that anger at the divorced parents is being directed toward playmates.
- *Development of new fears and phobias.* The preschool years are a time when even the most emotionally well-balanced child conjures up a host of fears, from monsters to spiders. How can you tell the difference between an age-appropriate fear and one that reflects emotional distress? Look for fears that seem out of character. If a child has always slept in a darkened room with the door closed but suddenly develops a phobia about sleeping with the lights out, you might suspect an underlying cause for the new fear. Another cause for concern is when a child who had will-ingly gone with a known caregiver or to a day-care center sud-denly becomes hysterical whenever the parent tries to leave.

- *Uncharacteristic sadness.* Preschoolers are usually filled with a curiosity and enthusiasm for life. If a youngster of this age loses that sense of wonder and becomes glum and weepy, it could signal the beginning of a depression.

If you see a pattern of these signs in a youngster that continues over time, or if the distress seems especially acute, bring it to the attention of your pediatrician. He or she will help you decide whether psychological counseling would be helpful and appropriate.

School-Age Children (Ages Six to Twelve)

School-age children have a much greater capacity than preschoolers to grasp abstract concepts, so they are more able to understand and imagine the consequences of their parents' divorce. They understand that the parents are no longer going to live together and that the new living arrangement will have an effect on their financial situation. However, these youngsters still have limitations on what they can grasp about the divorce, and their imagination fills the voids in their comprehension.

This is the age range when joint custody becomes an alternative. School-age children have a more mature concept of space and time and material belongings than preschoolers. They are able to understand that they have two homes and feel comfortable in each.

School-age children are still vulnerable to thinking that the divorce was caused by something they did. Such a point of view is understandable in many instances because the parents take their interpersonal fights into the child-rearing arena. Instead of the wife complaining, "You're never home with me," she may say, "You're the only father who doesn't go to the Little League games with your son." Thus the child sees himself as the focus of and the cause of family problems. He might imagine that if he weren't there, everything would be better. For that reason, children of this age might run away or, in extreme situations, attempt suicide.

School-age children also suffer a greater loss than their younger counterparts because they now have a sense of family that goes beyond the immediate household. They realize that they are losing not only their father in the divorce, but also their father's extended family of brothers, sisters, mother, and father. A whole family unit is being cut out of their life.

Crisis Stage

School-age youngsters of both sexes have fantasies of their parents' reconciling, just as younger children do. However, as they approach the age of nine, these children also begin to distinguish between their fantasies and the reality that there is nothing they can do to keep the family together. Their powerlessness in the divorce makes them feel helpless and then angry. Helplessness is such a terrible feeling that most children—most people, in fact—will turn it into anger at someone or something.

Boys and girls in this age group handle their anger in different ways. Boys tend to act out their anger. They may get into more fights at school, with friends, or with their sisters and brothers. Ironically, the people they're least likely to be angry with are their divorcing parents. The boys are terrified that they'll cause the remaining parent to walk out on them, too.

Girls tend to turn their anger around and become overly solicitous. They appear to be concerned and understanding, saying things like, "Mommy, I understand that you'll be much more happy after the divorce." Girls are praised for their helpfulness and understanding, and parents think that it's genuine. However, the anger is still there, lurking underneath the helpful facade. It eventually comes out— often during adolescence. This is usually a far worse time to deal with those angry feelings because teenage girls can act out their anger in much more dangerous ways—substance abuse, drinking, promiscuity—than school-age girls would.

Short-Term Stage

During this stage, the continuing parental conflict prevents school-age children from coming to terms with their parents' divorce. Their fears of abandonment are continually reawakened by their parents' ongoing fights.

In this stage, school-age children also may become increasingly sad and distressed before and after visits with the noncustodial parent. The custodial parent, seeing the child upset, often suggests that the child not visit the other parent anymore. The mother might say, "You get so upset when you see Dad. I don't think you should go there anymore." However, the child is not upset about *seeing* the noncustodial parent. She is upset about the loss of that parent and, if anything, needs to visit more often. A better response to the child's distress would be to say, "I know that you get sad when you see your Dad sometimes because it reminds you that the family is not the way it used to be. It's confusing, isn't it, that seeing someone can make you more aware of how much you don't see him? But these feelings will pass as you get used to visiting Daddy and feel that you can depend on your time with him."

Because of the continued fighting and loss of attention from the custodial parent, who is still making adjustments to the divorce herself, school-age children continue to be emotionally fragile and insecure during this stage of divorce. That insecurity causes these youngsters to postpone one of the developmental tasks of their age, which is to venture away from the family—make close friends on their own and develop close relationships with teachers. School-age children in the short-term stage of divorce don't have a secure enough home base to allow them to make these social forays into the outside world. Instead, they stay close to home, protecting what they see as their fragile support systems there.

Divorced parents inadvertently add to their school-age children's insecurity about going out into the world. Both parents are still too caught up in their own problems, or perhaps in a new romance, to notice much of what their children are doing. They don't offer the kind of praise that children need and deserve for taking steps toward independence. The children aren't rewarded for forging new relationships on their own, so they don't feel that their efforts have value.

At the same time, children of this age are old enough to help out around the house, and in a divorced household, the custodial parent may now ask for this help. She really needs it now that she's working full-time and can't afford help at home. School-age children feel big and important when they help out with necessary household duties like doing the laundry, washing dishes, shopping, and cleaning. However, all of these chores keep them tethered to the home at a time when they should be gaining a sense of independence and focusing their energy on relationships in the outside world.

Long-Term Stage

When considering the school-age child in the long-term stage of divorce, keep in mind the age of the child when the divorce first occurred. The child whose parents divorced when he was four will face different issues than the child whose parents divorced when she was ten.

If a child was a preschooler when his parents divorced, he probably has few memories of his intact family. At this point, his relationship with the custodial parent is very intense, whereas that with the noncustodial parent may be distant or nonexistent if, as happens in most cases, the father visits less and less frequently.

However, if the divorce occurred when a child was ten, she will have vivid memories of her life with an intact family. The child may have come to accept the changes in her life that resulted from the divorce, but she still feels the loss of the time when Mom and Dad lived together.

In the long-term stage of divorce, it's not uncommon for the custodial parent to be dating regularly or even remarrying. For the school-age child, the remarriage has several consequences.

- Forced awareness of their parents' sexuality may be uncomfortable for children of this age. School-age children are old enough to know that their parents had sex to have children. If the parents are married, however, there's little overt sexuality between them, and the children can deny their parents' sexual relationship. Sex is still "yucky" to kids of this age. However, when Mom is falling in love and the new man in her life is always grabbing her around the waist and kissing her, it's hard to avoid noticing that she's sexually active.

- The new romantic interest in the mother's life takes away some of her intense focus on her children, which will make the relationship more normal. However, the children will experience the shared attention as a loss.

- Children don't always like the mother's choice for a new partner, and that can set the stage for a lot of tension as well as feelings of competition.

- If the noncustodial parent dates and marries, he may give up even his occasional visits to the children and vanish completely from their lives. This is particularly true when his new partner has children or when he and his new wife begin a new family. School-age children are obviously aware of the waning interest of the noncustodial parent but are powerless to do anything to change it.

Signs of Distress

All of this domestic turmoil affects school-age children emotionally and interferes with their development. The developmental tasks that school-age children need to achieve include taking the first independent steps away from home by making their own friends, developing close relationships with teachers, getting involved in after-school activities, having sleep-overs at a friend's house, or going away to camp. School-age children in the long-term stage of divorce often put off these steps toward independence. They may develop solitary activities that they do at home, such as playing video games, organizing card or doll collections, or playing on the computer. Although these are normal activities for school-age kids, in the case of divorced kids of this age they can take the place of peer relationships and activities.

Some kids feel outwardly sad and depressed, but more often they turn their anger at their divorced parents toward peers and siblings, often overreacting to real or imagined slights.

Children might also show signs of general anxiety, such as nervous habits like nail-biting. Girls, in particular, tend to develop physical complaints like headaches and stomachaches.

Teenagers (Ages Twelve to Eighteen)

Parents often feel that once children hit the teenage years, they'll be more able to handle a divorce than they would have been earlier, but the opposite is true. Adolescence appears to be the worst time in a child's life for parents to divorce. Such a decision at that time forces the child to handle two very difficult changes in life: (1) all of the physical and emotional changes that arise during the teen years and (2) the emotional distress of a divorce.

Adolescents, more than school-age children, need a secure home base as they think about going out into the world by choosing a college and a career. Because they need to know that their home will be there for them to return to, threatening that home is very upsetting to teenagers.

Another reason this can be a particularly bad time in a child's life for parents to divorce is that adolescents are capable of acting out their feelings in ways that are much more harmful to themselves.

Rather than being the class clown and being sent to the principal's office, teens are more likely to get involved in petty crime, sexual promiscuity, irresponsible driving, or substance abuse. Parents who are divorcing and in the midst of their own turmoil are not as likely to notice signs of trouble in their teenagers until a great deal of damage has already been done.

In addition to this more dangerous behavior, teens show many of the same signs of distress as younger children. Their academic performance falters. They get into more squabbles with their peers and other family members. They also have difficulty achieving the central developmental tasks of their age group, which are furthering their independence from home and beginning relationships with the opposite sex. Children who lose their intact family are burdened with the sense that a loving relationship can end at any time. They live with a high degree of anxiety over being betrayed by a romantic partner, which makes starting a love relationship difficult. This hesitancy to make themselves vulnerable in a love relationship often continues well into adulthood when children of divorced families find themselves reluctant to make a commitment to marriage for fear that it won't last and they will be hurt.

Crisis Stage

When initially faced with their parents' decision to divorce, teenagers react with shock. They feel overwhelmed by their emotions. The home that they have always relied on is coming apart. The stable family that teens have depended on to show them important values and rules is unraveling. The parents are turning the rules upside down by saying, "Well, we don't feel good about each other now, so we're going to break up." This decision is in direct contradiction to what most teens imagine family to mean. Family should always be there. It is the one trusted base that teens feel they should be able to rely on, and divorce takes that away.

For the kids in this age group, divorce causes a rapid shift in their feelings and perceptions about their parents. Instead of Dad being a hard-working person who would do anything for the family, he is now the jerk who is leaving Mom to live with his twenty-five-year-old secretary. This sudden change in attitude affects one of the important developmental tasks of the teen years: the development of a realistic view of the parent as a person separate from the parent as parent. Usually, teens begin to see both the strong and the weak sides of their parents, and they integrate what they see into a mature image of who their parents are. As Mark Twain is alleged to have said, "The older I got, the smarter my parents got." Divorce interrupts that process and forces a much more polarized view of the parents. Usually, Mom is the martyr, and Dad is the bad guy.

Teens faced with divorce regress to a self-centered attitude wherein they believe that they are somehow the cause of the breakup. They might think, "I smashed up the car and that made Dad so mad, it was the last straw for him," or "I didn't obey my curfew once again, only this time Mom and Dad ended up fighting over me, and now they're getting divorced." You might think that teenagers should be mature enough to know better than to think that they caused the divorce, but remember that adolescence is a time of self-absorption. Teens, like their younger preschool counterparts, put themselves at the center of the universe. They think that people stare at them, that teachers target them for criticism in class, and that they could create enough discord between their parents to cause a divorce. You have to let your teen know that isn't the truth.

Divorce also has a negative effect on a teen's self-esteem. Teens are so sensitive about everything that even a small pimple is a terrible thing. What does it mean when their parents separate? It may mean that the parents don't love them. It may mean that they weren't good enough children. It could take on any number of negative connotations, all of which take a toll on the child's sense of self.

Another difficult part of the crisis stage of divorce is the custody dispute. Younger children are told where they will live, but teens may be asked with whom they prefer to live. They find it hard to choose or even honestly say whom they prefer. By doing so, they feel that they are betraying the parent they don't choose. They feel that they would be engendering anger and bitterness in the noncustodial parent, no matter how much reassurance they hear to the contrary. How can a child risk alienating a parent in that way?

Short-Term Stage

For teenagers, the consequences of the crisis stage of divorce continue into the short term. The shock is gone now, but the feelings of responsibility and betrayal of the noncustodial parent continue. These feelings may even be intensified if the child is used as a go-between and confidant for the parents. This happens even more with this age group than with younger children because teens are seen as being more responsible. Teens may be more capable, but they are also more alert to their role. Thus, teens who are used as spies and messengers for their divorced parents often feel guilty about their role but are unable to say no to their parents.

For teenage sons, there is the additional burden of sexual tension between son and mother. This is a normal part of growing up for boys, but when there is a father, the tension is diffused. Also, the married mother is not as overtly sexual as she is when she's newly single and looking to attract dates. Her heightened sexuality is difficult for a son to deal with when his own sexual awareness is becoming acute.

Long-Term Stage

Teens are just as likely as younger children to have fantasies of their parents' reuniting. During the long-term stage, they understand better than younger children the significance of Mom's dating and Dad's buying another home, and they are particularly alarmed by any such parental behavior that might signify that the divorce is permanent.

Signs of Distress

Because the teen years are tumultuous in themselves and because teens have a much greater awareness of what transpires between their divorcing parents, the emotional toll of divorce on adolescents remains acute for longer than with younger children. Parents—married or divorced—expect their teenagers to behave erratically at best, so how can a divorced parent tell whether her adolescent is suffering emotionally because of the divorce or whether the child is just going through "a phase"? The clue is in the degree of the behavior. It's normal for your teenage daughter to be best friends with a girl one day and hate her the next, but if she is fighting with all of her peers, something is awry. Excessive drinking and promiscuous sex are also warning signs. Another warning sign is a significant change in academic performance. It's normal for a child to have weaknesses academically or, in the aftermath of a divorce, even to have a bad semester; but if a teen is failing everything, it's time to call in professional help.

TELLING YOUR CHILD

Prepare your child for the separation by sitting down and telling him or her your intentions. Don't wait until the movers pull up to take away the belongings of one parent, but don't tell the child six months in advance of the real separation either. Letting your child know a couple of weeks before the household is broken up is usually plenty of advance notice.

If it is at all possible, parents should explain their decision to divorce together. This sends the message that the decision is a mutual one, not one that is being forced on one partner by the other and certainly not one for which the child is responsible.

DEBRIEFING FOR DIVORCE

Because we now know that divorce is not always better in the long run for the children, parents are even more reluctant to separate, and many work harder to find some compromise that will allow them to keep the family intact. However, parents who feel that divorce is unavoidable can still help their children handle the turmoil, sort through their feelings about the breakup of their family, and develop better coping skills by using the four-step debriefing method outlined in Chapter 4, as shown here.

Debriefing can be used during the crisis stage, when you make the decision to divorce, and again as the child enters new stages of the divorce process and develops a more mature understanding of what the decision to divorce meant. A five-year-old will have different questions about why Daddy is moving away from home than a teenager will.

When is the right time to repeat the debriefing? When you are about to make any major change, such as moving to a new home or getting married, or when the children start to ask new questions about why you decided to break up the family. You don't necessarily have to go through all of the steps each time you debrief. Sometimes one or two steps are all that is needed.

Step I: Preparing Yourself

If you have read through this chapter, you have already done the homework you need to prepare for the divorce debriefing. The chapter will make you familiar with the three stages of divorce and the effects of age and gender on a child's reaction to divorce.

If you are so distraught and unhinged by the divorce that you can't talk calmly and reassuringly to the children, have a friend or relative do the debriefing for you. If you try to talk to the children when you are very upset, they will hesitate to express their own feelings of hurt and anger because they won't want to burden you with them. One of the important parts of the debriefing is to give the children an opportunity to air their feelings. However, showing some emotion is appropriate. It would be abnormal for you to be unemotional about getting divorced.

If you have more than one child, debrief all of the children at one time. Children of different ages support one another. Older children can explain things to younger children later if there was something that the young ones didn't understand.

The following are several important points that you should know when preparing for a debriefing. Remember, this is a stressful time for you too, so take care of yourself.

- *Be prepared to assure the children that they had nothing to do with the decision.*   They are not the cause of the divorce, nor can they do anything that will change the decision. Tell them that you have already tried to find any number of ways to work out your differences before coming to this decision and none of them worked.
- *Remember to be honest and straightforward.*   Don't make false promises. If children ask questions for which you don't have an answer, say "I don't know." Don't make up an answer to assuage their anxiety. Just let them know that you'll be talking to them as the situation changes and decisions are made.
- *Do not blame one another or put one another down in front of the children, even if you are angry at each other.*   For the kids' sake, keep your gripes about one another to yourselves.
- *Be prepared to tell the children what they can expect if you know what is going to happen in the near future.*   Fill in as many details as possible: Daddy will be moving to a new home a few blocks away. We are going to move in with Grandma for a while. Mommy's going to have a new job, and you'll have a new babysitter. Daddy's going to take the television, but we're going to get a new one. Instead of me taking you to school, you'll be taking the bus with your friends.
- *Stress the things that will not change.*   You will be staying right here, although Daddy will be moving away. Mommy will be taking

a job, but she will still be able to be with you after school (or, Mommy will be taking a new job, and the baby-sitter who is usually here only on Tuesdays and Thursdays will be here every day when you get home from school).

- *Be prepared to answer the questions the children* don't *ask, too.*   The children may be too dumbstruck to know what to ask. Put yourself in their shoes, and think about what questions you would have if you were in their position. Aim to alleviate any anxieties you imagine they might have. Think about their daily routine. What will change? What will stay the same?
- *Reassure, reassure, reassure.*   Mommy and Daddy don't love each other anymore. We're not happy together anymore, but we both love you, and that won't change. We will always be your parents, and we're going to work together even if we're living apart.

It's good to let the children know that you did once love each other and that you think it's very sad that your love has changed. Let them know that you are aware that your decision is hurtful to them and that you know it will make them sad. Your saying this will give them permission to cry and be upset.

Managing your own stress and adapting quickly to your new life will make the divorce less stressful for the children. Initially, custodial parents are at first distraught, but then they immerse themselves in the single life to get back into the swing of things after their years of marriage. These activities make custodial parents less available to their children. As they come to terms with their divorce, custodial parents usually balance their new social needs more evenly with the needs of their children, and they are able to focus more on their children again.

Step II: Having the Child Tell the Story

In a debriefing following a separation, not only do the children tell the story, but the parents recount their experiences, too.

- *Let the children know how difficult this decision was to make.* Tell the children that you understand that the decision is painful for them as well as for yourselves. Tell them that you didn't make the decision easily, but only after realizing that you can no longer live together either because you no longer love one another or because you can't stop fighting. It's okay to give the children a reason why you're breaking up. In fact, the divorce will make more sense if children are told why it is happening. However, some details are best left out, such as sexual problems or infidelity.

- *Help the children talk about their feelings by remembering and sharing family history.* You might say, for instance, "Do you remember when we all used to go to the movies? I miss that." Statements like this encourage the children to talk about their favorite family activities and what they will miss. Children might also talk about how the arguments between their parents spoiled some of their family outings, and that's important to hear, too.

  What you hear from children will depend on their age, their gender, and the stage of the divorce. With preschool and young school-age children, for instance, you might need to start this step by saying, "I want to tell you again that Mommy and Daddy are not going to live together anymore. Daddy has a new house." Then the child can say, "Yes, Daddy's far away, and I miss him." With all children, a good way to get this step going is to say, "Do you remember . . . ," and recount a family story or situation that will help the children understand the divorce better or will get them to express their feelings of hurt and anger.

- *Remember that it's hard for children to talk about their feelings concerning a divorce.* You are the cause of their pain, and they find it hard to come out and say, "I hate you. You did this terrible thing to me." If you lead the way, however, by talking about your painful feelings, they'll be more likely to be open with theirs. If you say, "Now that we're getting separated, Daddy and I won't be fighting in front of you anymore. I always hated it when that happened." Then the child might respond by saying, "Yes. I don't like it when Daddy comes home from work and you start to argue right away."

  If you do this step in a repeat debriefing, perhaps in the beginning of the short-term stage of the divorce, you might start out by saying, "I told you things would get better after I had a chance to figure things out. Now I want to check in with you and see how you are and what *still* needs to get done." In this way, you're telling the children that you're trying to make things better, but you're leaving the door open for them to tell you what is still bothering them.

Step III: Sharing the Child's Reaction

In this third step, an important goal is helping the children understand that their feelings of anger, guilt, and loss as well as their school
problems and other reactionary behaviors are normal. It's normal to
miss family get-togethers, especially on holidays like Mother's Day,
Father's Day, Thanksgiving, or seasonal holidays.

- *Tell the children some of the reactions you've noticed.*   For instance, you might say, "You've been staying in your room a lot
  since the separation. I guess the house seems very different now,"
  or, "You seem very sad when you come back from Daddy's house,
  and I'm wondering if you miss him a lot?"
- *Give the children permission to say what they are feeling.*
  Sometimes children are afraid to talk about their unhappy reactions because they don't want to make their parents feel bad. One
  way to give them permission to talk about their feelings is to
  express your own. You might say, "Sometimes I miss the way
  things used to be. Do you?"
- *Help them look for some solutions to problems that have arisen
  since the separation.*   You might say, "Sometimes kids have a
  hard time thinking about their schoolwork after a divorce. Maybe
  that's why you're having trouble at school. Maybe there is some
  way I can help, or maybe I can get someone else to help you for
  a little while." By offering to help, you become not only a part
  of the problem (one of the people who decided to get a divorce),
  but also a part of the solution.
- *Accept your children's point of view of the divorce.*   You might
  believe that there was no option but to get a divorce, but your
  children probably don't see it that way. Your job in this step is to
  look at the situation from the children's point of view and hear
  that point of view from them without getting defensive.

Step IV: Survival and Recovery

The most difficult task for children of divorced families is to make
a commitment to a loving relationship in adulthood. They fear that
a divorce could tear their marriage and home life apart at any moment. You can counter that reaction in the following ways:

- *Express concern for your ex-spouse at appropriate times.* If, for instance, you hear through the children that their father is sick, avoid saying, "Who cares?" The children care a great deal. Even when spouses didn't get along while married, that doesn't mean that they can't have a relationship in which they express concern for each other when they are separated. Examples like this go a long way toward helping children feel that relationships can last even if love ends.

- *Support visitation not only with the noncustodial parent, but with the noncustodial parent's extended family.* Telephone calls, letters, sending scrapbooks to grandparents, and visits help maintain attachments after a divorce. This will help children see that family relationships can transcend the dissolution of a marriage and will make it easier for them to take a chance on love later. Being civil or sometimes even kind to a divorced spouse is difficult, especially after very contentious marriages or bitter divorces. However, keep in mind that this is one of the few ways that you can undo the damage done by the divorce.

9

ILLNESS AND INJURY

Coping with the Unexpected

Illness and injury are dreaded in parents' lives and frightening to children, particularly if an injury is not accidental, but purposefully inflicted by someone else. How can you reassure a child who is recovering from an accidental injury? How can you talk to a child about a parent or even a friend, classmate, or pet who is seriously ill or who was hurt in an act of violence? In this chapter, you'll find tools you can use in talking to your child about illness or injury, but first, here's some information that you should have about what happens to people when an illness or injury befalls them.

WHAT YOU SHOULD KNOW ABOUT ILLNESS AND INJURY

When a serious illness is diagnosed or an injury occurs, teams of medical specialists use the latest technology to bring the patient through a medical crisis that might have been fatal just a few years ago. While we are thankful for what seems to be a medical miracle, we now have to face horrific treatments and long convalescences that can be as hard to cope with as the original illness or injury.

- While caring for an ill or injured loved one during a prolonged convalescence, we are often so overwhelmed that we feel frustrated and exhausted rather than grateful, and then we feel guilty.

- After a serious illness or injury, we may feel reassured that the person will survive, but we often don't know how full a recovery we can expect. Will the loved one walk and move around the same way? Will she talk and joke and remember as she used to? Will he be the same person he was before the accident?

- When an adult is ill or seriously injured, the family routine is totally disrupted. Everyone's attention turns to help the sick or injured person recover. Other relatives come and take over the housework and child-care responsibilities. Schedules are re-arranged to allow for hospital visits. Children often find themselves left with baby-sitters or dropped off with relatives rather than having the time at home with their families that they are used to.

- The ill person often changes physically and emotionally. She may look drawn and ill, and she may be cantankerous or, conversely, lackluster and unresponsive.

- When a child is ill, household routines often have to be abandoned, too. Arrangements have to be made for a parent or close relative to leave work to be with the child. Dinner might come at 10 P.M. after hospital visiting hours instead of after returning home from work. Parents may hardly see each other or their other children as they take turns being with the sick child.

- Like adults, ill or injured children may change physically and emotionally when they go through painful or debilitating treatments. Some withdraw; some become angry and uncooperative.

- Brothers and sisters may feel a mix of concern for their sibling and jealousy for all of the attention being paid to him or her at their expense. Then they feel guilty for their jealousy.

- All of these feelings can be complicated by anger and fear when the injury is a result of malicious intent or random violence, such as in the case of the Oklahoma City bombing or a shooting during a robbery. There is anger at the person who caused the injury, fear of being hurt again, and concern that someone else in the family could be a victim, too.

- In cases of injury caused by violence, the family may become the focus of media attention or may become involved with the criminal justice system, both of which are disruptive and invasive to the family.

HOW CHILDREN REACT WHEN THEY ARE ILL OR INJURED

Four-year-old Henry had a hearing problem and went into the hospital for a day to have his adenoids removed to improve his hearing. His mother said that he was going to go to sleep during the operation and that she would be there when he awoke. However, during the first few minutes after he was brought back to consciousness and moved into the recovery room, Mom wasn't there. By the time she was allowed into his room, Henry was hysterical.

Shortly after this minor procedure, Henry developed an infection and had to go back to the hospital for a lot of tests. He was so terrified about going back to the hospital that three months later, he was still talking about the operation and the tests and asking if he was going to get any more "pinches" (shots or blood tests). He was terrified both because his mother wasn't there when he woke up—he feared being abandoned—and because of the hospital experience itself.

The wonderful thing about this story is that Henry could hear much better after the surgery, but the outcome didn't seem wonderful for Henry. He was just terrified that he might have to go back for more medical treatments.

Younger Children (Ages Two to Nine)

Medical procedures required to treat an illness or injury are frightening for children. Young children like Henry are particularly traumatized by treatments and tests that hurt them, such as shots, IVs, getting blood drawn, or spinal taps. These preschool and school-age children don't understand what is happening to them or why these things are being done to them.

Adults know that children are afraid of medical procedures, and often their first response is to be secretive about what is wrong with the child and what will happen during treatment. Even young children, however, can and need to prepare themselves as best they can for something that will pinch or hurt, so don't try to hide what is going on from your child. Explain in as simple terms as necessary that she is sick and that the doctors are going to help her get better. When something is going to hurt, warn the child and reassure her that you'll be there to comfort her. Younger children should be told about what is going to happen to them no more than 24 hours in advance, but at least a few hours, before any medical procedures or hospitalization. In other words, there should be enough time to prepare by talking, reading books, and so on, but not time to dwell unnecessarily.

Sometimes preschool and young school-age children become withdrawn when they are ill or injured. They may even refuse or fight treatment because they don't understand that it will ultimately help them. They already feel sick and hurt, and then some strangers come in and hurt them even more. They feel powerless in this situation, and one way to gain control is to try to stop the hurtful things from happening again.

Children in this age group need to be reassured that they'll be all right. Adults may be frightened by having a painful attack of appendicitis, but they know that once the appendix is out they'll be okay. Children don't know that. They may panic, thinking that this terrible pain and the rush to the hospital mean that they are going to die. In situations where your child will be okay, you need to reassure him that he'll be perfectly normal again after he recovers.

Even with preparation, children are likely to continue to have fears. As in Henry's case, youngsters may constantly worry about having to go through painful medical procedures again. Repeated, patient reassurance that they won't have those experiences again, along with the passage of time as proof, will help assuage their fears.

When a child is ill, she is isolated from her world. She can't go to school or play or hang out with her friends. She may feel that she's losing her place among her peers as they move on in day care or school. The child may feel as if her peers will see her as being different because she has been ill or injured. Those feelings make it hard for the child to return to normal activities after recovery.

What about the child who is not going to be all right, who is not going to recover or recover fully? This child also needs honest answers about his condition, about what his treatment will be, and about the gravity of his illness or injury. There's no need to go into gory details unnecessarily, but it's also unwise to hide the truth from children. If they are old enough to communicate, children need you to be truthful in answering their questions about what will happen to them. They need to know what they can expect their lives to be like so that they can come to terms with their illness or injury, face some of their fears, and do the things they want to do while they are able. Remember, a child's imaginings of what will happen may be far worse than the reality of what is to come.

Imagination, in fact, plays a large role in how young children view their illness or injury. Most young children believe that if you're good, good things will happen to you. If they become ill or injured, they may believe that they somehow deserved it, that they were bad in some way. It's important to let your child know that she isn't to blame for her illness or injury, that these things just happen sometimes, and that you and the doctors are doing everything possible to help her get better.

Older Children (Ages Ten to Eighteen)

Older school-age children and teenagers have a far more sophisticated understanding of the implications of an illness or injury, and this is a mixed blessing. On the one hand, older children can understand much more of what is happening and why. On the other hand, they have much more mature concerns and fears about the outcome of their condition. You should talk to your older child or teenager about uncommon medical procedures within a time frame that recognizes their emotional and cognitive abilities, so that they have enough time to come to terms with the situation.

Children in this age group are particularly sensitive to illnesses or injuries that would cause them to look different from their peers. Hair loss caused by chemotherapy for cancer, for instance, is distressing for everyone, but for teens, it's particularly traumatic because it will make them look dramatically different from their peers. Reassure them often that the hair loss is only temporary and that their hair will grow back once the chemotherapy is over.

These children are less anxious about going through medical procedures, such as having blood drawn or getting shots. These kids can understand why the procedures are being done and that they are usually finished in a short period of time.

Children in this age group also have a far better grasp on how their illness or injury will affect them. They can understand time frames better, so they will know how long it will take before they can get back to normal. They can also understand the concept of chronic conditions, and they can use their understanding to make the physical and psychological adjustments that are necessary to return to a normal life, compensating for their medical condition.

For all of their maturity, older school-age children and teens nevertheless feel the terrible frustration of being powerless. They may not refuse or fight treatment as younger children may, but they will act out. They may get involved in risky behavior or do things that they know may set back or compromise their recovery. This is their way of trying to gain some control over the situation.

HOW CHILDREN REACT WHEN ADULTS ARE ILL OR INJURED

Children are frightened when the adults in their lives are ill or injured. If it is one of the parents or primary caregivers, youngsters fear that one of the people who cares for and protects them can't provide that care and that someone they love very much is so seriously ill or hurt that he or she has to be taken away or put to bed. The other parent's attention is also elsewhere, focused on getting the sick or injured person well again.

If the ill or injured person is another adult in the family, the children might not find the situation as immediately threatening, but they are still concerned and may be frightened by seeing their parents worry and by the changes they see in the ill or injured person.

Unfortunately, the children's feelings and fears are often not the center of attention when an adult family member becomes incapacitated. The immediate concerns are helping the sick person get medical care and reorganizing household and work routines to accommodate the sick or injured person's treatment and convalescence. Children may be shuttled to someone else's house or put in a baby-sitter's care. Once the basic needs of the kids are met, the adults focus on the convalescing family member. What often gets forgotten is how the children are understanding and coping with the abrupt changes in their lives and the loved one's condition.

A friend told me this story: Her mother-in-law was living with her while she was in the process of getting her own apartment. One morning, the mother-in-law appeared to have overslept, but when my friend went in, she found that the woman had had a stroke in the middle of the night. Of course, my friend and her husband rushed the woman to the hospital, leaving their twelve-year-old son asleep in the next room. When he woke up, he found a wet spot in Grandma's empty bed and no one at home. He was both terrified and angry at his parents for leaving him alone without any explanation. The parents came home eventually and told their son what had happened. He could see how upset they were, so he didn't mention how angry he was. In fact, his parents never thought about nor were they aware of his feelings that morning until fifteen years later when the event came up in conversation. "I didn't tell you how mad I was at you for leaving me alone like that because you were so distressed and I didn't want to burden you," he finally told them.

This situation isn't uncommon. When someone is seriously ill or injured, we don't even think about the children except to make sure that they are somewhere safe. We shouldn't berate ourselves for behaving this way during these critical times. However, once the immediate crisis is past, we should try to see the situation through our children's eyes and address their feelings. The four-step debriefing method at the end of this chapter is a good tool for this.

Younger Children (Ages Two to Nine)

When someone is seriously ill or injured, the adults are distressed, and youngsters are very attuned to that. Preschoolers and young school-age children are aware of the distress, but they have no way to label or express what they are witnessing. They may act out or become distressed themselves, be clingy or moody, or show other signs of distress.

Young children use their magical thinking to try to make the sickness go away. Three-year-old Tim tried to make his mommy better by pulling at the intravenous lines in her arms. He thought that they were hurting her and that if he took them out he would make her better. Children's magical thinking can make them feel that they somehow caused the illness or injury. If a young child got angry at her mother, she might believe that her angry thoughts made her mother have an accident and hurt herself. Of course, these children need to be reassured that they in no way caused the illness or injury.

Older Children (Ages Ten to Eighteen)

Older school-age children and teenagers are much more aware of what an illness or injury is and the consequences of an adult being seriously ill. They worry more about the adult's recovery. Will he be the same? How long will it take? Will he be in pain? Will the illness come back?

Older children also understand the financial consequences if a breadwinner in the family is too ill or injured to work. They may ask questions about whether there is enough money for food or to keep the house. They may not ask for things that they usually want, such as shoes, games, or summer camp, because they worry that the family can't afford it. They need to be informed about the financial welfare of the family and whether they'll be able to have the things they're used to, or what they might have to give up.

Like their younger counterparts, older children sometimes wonder if they are in some way responsible for the adult's illness. Did they worry Dad so much that he had a heart attack? Did they cause Mom so much stress that she wasn't thinking about her driving and had a car accident? It's important to reassure the children that nothing they did caused the illness or injury. No one is at fault. These things just happen in life.

Another aspect of having an ill or injured relative that greatly disturbs kids of this age is all of the attention that they get from others, being pointed out by friends and teachers and given sympathy for having a sick family member. Rather than making them feel supported, all of this attention makes them feel stigmatized and embarrassed.

Bringing Children to the Hospital

Children miss the sick or injured relative, whether it's a parent, sibling, or grandparent. They worry about them and want to see them. You might be concerned about the child being frightened or upset by seeing the family member in the hospital. Hospitals have varying policies concerning the age of visitors, but if your child is allowed to visit, it's generally all right to bring him as long as you tell him what to expect and make sure that he wants to go after he's heard what he might see. Let your child know that Daddy may be sleepy and connected by tubes to various machines. Tell him that Mommy's going to have a big bandage and may not be feeling very well. If the child is still anxious to visit, give the patient some notice and take the child in with you.

Once you're at the hospital, follow the child's lead. If he just wants to look for a minute and then wait out in the hall, let him. Don't insist that he give the patient a kiss. The child may only want to hold the patient's hand, or he may not want to touch the person at all.

When the visit is over, talk to the child about what he saw and how he felt. Ask if he has any questions or feelings that he wants to share with you. Ask about the smells and sounds of the hospital visit. Although seemingly incidental to the visit, they have a powerful effect on unconscious memory.

DEBRIEFING FOR ILLNESS AND INJURY

Chapter 4 describes the basic concept and four steps of the debriefing method. Reviewing that information will give you the background you need to talk with your child. Here are some ideas to tailor the process so it will be most effective in helping your child overcome the trauma caused by an illness or injury.

Step I: Preparing Yourself

To help your children grasp what is happening, you have to understand the situation yourself.

* *Make sure that you learn everything you can about the accident, injury, or illness; the treatment options; and the predicted outcome for the patient.* Don't be shy about asking the doctors, nurses, and hospital social workers for information. If the injury was due to an act of violence, find out as much as you can about the incident and how the person was injured.

    It sometimes becomes apparent that an illness or injury will ultimately lead to death. Once that outcome is known, you need to be informed about how much time and what quality of life the patient can expect.

- *Find out how to talk to children about an impending death.*   If a child is not expected to survive an illness or injury, you'll need to know the best way to talk about that with her. Different children should be told in different ways, depending on their age and their condition. Before talking with your child, consult a physician, religious leader, hospital social worker, or professional counselor. These are all good sources who will be able to tell you how to address different aspects of the situation with the child. The other family members also need to be informed, and these same professionals can help you find the best way to talk to them.
- *Help yourself emotionally.*   This is one of the most important parts of preparing to debrief a child. Children will find it reassuring if you're calm and assured. Think about whether you feel guilt or blame for the person being ill or injured. If you've agreed to treatments suggested by doctors that haven't turned out as successfully as expected, do you blame yourself for making that decision? If you're distraught, talk about your concerns to a doctor, hospice worker, social worker, or religious leader. These are the people who can help you get information and come to terms with the choices you've made.

    If you find that you are overwhelmed by your responsibility for caring for the patient or by your own grief, think about whether you have the patience and time to do a debriefing now. If you do not, help a friend or relative prepare to do it in your place.

Step II: Having the Child Tell the Story

When there is an illness or injury in the family, the child is usually shielded from information about what is wrong with the patient—even when the child herself is the ill or injured party! All she has to go on are repeated reassurances that everything is going to be all right, and dribs and drabs of conversations overheard between adults. The child fills in these odd bits of real information with her imagination, which can make the situation better or worse than it really is but certainly won't help her cope with the reality of the illness or injury that is affecting her and her family. Children need to know the truth about what is happening so that they, too, can prepare emotionally for convalescence or a possible death.

- *Tell the story from the beginning.*   You may do the debriefing after the initial crisis of the accident or the diagnosis of the illness has passed. When you tell the story, back up and begin talking about how the injury occurred or when the symptoms of the illness were first noticed.

- *Ask your child what he has heard about the illness or injury.* If it is the child who is ill or injured, let him tell you what he heard about his condition from doctors and family members. You might say, "You saw Mom and Dad talking to your doctor. What did you hear? That's a strange big word. What do you think it means?" Avoid "Do you know . . ." questions. These are easily answered with a one-word answer that doesn't help you understand how the child is thinking or whether what he's thinking is correct. Questions that begin with "what . . ." and "how . . ." allow the child to tell you about his ideas.

  When an adult is ill or injured, children are often given a brief, unsatisfying description of what is wrong that leaves them with many questions that they're afraid to ask. Find out what your child knows. Ask, "What questions do you have?" Say, "Mom will help you get the answers you need."

- *Find out about the treatments your child has had, has heard about, or has seen.*   If the child has been ill or injured, let her talk about the treatments she's had or has heard she is going to have. Was she prepared for what was going to happen? Were the treatments painful? Does she have any questions about what is being done to her and why?

  If it is an adult who is being treated, find out what the child knows is being done to help the person, and answer any questions about what other medical steps might be taken. Let the child know why these treatments are necessary and provide some time frame for the course of treatment if possible.

- *Talk about changes in the ill or injured person.*   Does the child feel that her illness or injury has changed her? Did the treatment make her feel different? Has she lost weight or lost her hair?

  You'll want the same information about how your child sees an injured or ill adult. What differences has she noticed in the adult? Does she know why the changes are occurring?

  After talking about the changes, give the child as much information as possible about when things will get back to normal. Tell her that hair loss due to chemotherapy is temporary and the hair will grow back. Let her know that she'll be able to walk normally again once the cast is taken off and she's had some treatment to strengthen the leg. Tell her that Dad will be tired and weak for a few weeks but then will feel better than he did before he was ill.

- *Find out if the child has noticed any change in attitude toward the patient from caregivers or family and friends.* Has the behavior of people toward the ill or injured person changed over time? Have family and friends become less patient and less attentive? Has the child noticed that the doctors and nurses were positive at first but now seem less hopeful? Help the child understand why these changes in people's behavior are taking place.

Step III: Sharing the Child's Reaction

The goal of this step is to give your child permission to talk to you about what is happening to him and how he feels about it, especially since some or all of it hasn't been pleasant. Whether he is the patient or a close relative of the patient, the child's life has been disrupted.

- *If the injury was a result of an act of violence, let the child know that wanting revenge is normal.* Fantasizing revenge against someone who hurt you or someone you love is normal. Let the child know that he shouldn't feel guilty for having these thoughts or other angry feelings toward the person who caused the injury.
- *Find out about the child's fears concerning the injured adult.* If an adult is severely injured or gravely ill, a child may fear that she'll be abandoned by that person. She may be worrying that the adult will die. If you can reassure the child with certainty that the adult will recover, do so. However, if the adult may die, be honest. You can say something like, "The doctors are doing everything they can to make Daddy better, but we really don't know now if he's going to get all better." If the adult is well enough to be at home or to be visited in the hospital, you can add, "Even though Daddy's sick, he's still part of the family, and we can still spend time with him." Talk to the doctor, hospital social worker, hospice personnel, and your religious leader about the most appropriate way to approach your child.

- *Find out the child's reactions to his own illness and treatments.* Children who are seriously ill and go through therapies like chemotherapy during which they feel sick and lose their hair, or who are severely injured and have to wear braces or casts, feel different and isolated from peers and family. They may worry that the family may not love them the way they are or that friends may shun them. This, unfortunately, may not all be in their imaginations. People do avoid those who are sick or infirm.

  You can reassure your child by explaining that people get scared when their loved ones and friends are sick and that sometimes that fear makes them act strange for a little while. Reassure the child that "Mom, Dad, and Grandpa love you with or without your hair." Also, arrange to have good friends visit as soon as the child is well enough, even if she looks a little different or is wearing a cast or brace. Prepare the friends in advance by telling them how the child will look different so they won't be shocked when they see her.

  If the child may not recover and she's old enough to understand that, don't be afraid to talk about the subject. It's certainly something that she's thinking about a lot. Again, talk to the doctor, your religious leader, hospital social worker, and professional counselor about the most appropriate words to use to talk to the child. Ask about the child's feelings concerning the treatments she is going through, and find out her thoughts and fears about the possibility of dying.

- *Let children know that feelings of anger and jealousy are normal.* Children of all ages wonder why *their* mom, dad, or grandparent got sick or why *they* got sick. They may feel jealous of other kids who aren't burdened with a sick or injured relative or who don't have a health problem, and then they feel guilty over having those jealous feelings. Let your child know that such feelings are normal and nothing to be ashamed about.

Step IV: Survival and Recovery

- *Keep the child involved in his normal life to whatever extent possible during treatment and recuperation.* If the child is seriously ill or injured, his limitations should be explained and reinforced so that he doesn't inadvertently cause himself a setback, but the more he begins to feel a part of things again, the easier his transition back to normal life will be once he's recovered and the higher his morale will be. If the child can't play with his soccer team this year, find some other sport in which he can participate.

- *Ask the child's doctor or hospital social worker about local support groups that help children with health problems similar to your child's.* Being with children who have survived similar illnesses or injuries will boost the child's morale and may also help her learn new skills that she may need to resume a normal life.

    Similar steps should be taken for adults who are convalescing. Rather than have the adult withdraw, try to involve him in as many of his usual family activities as possible. Dad may not be able to coach the soccer team for the season, but he can come to the games in a wheelchair and cheer his daughter on.

- *Protect children from media intrusion.* If an act of violence was the cause of injury for the child or adult, reporters may call and come to the home to get information or reactions from the family. Shield children from the media as much as possible. This includes turning off the evening news when the crime report is aired.

- *Limit your child's exposure to the criminal justice system.* If the child's injury was the result of a violent crime, do your best to limit the child's nonessential involvement in the legal proceedings. Testifying in court and being questioned by police are frightening to children and only adds to the trauma of being the victim of a violent crime. Find out if your child has to be interviewed and where. Can a parent be present? Can it be done at home? Can it be taped so that the interview doesn't have to be repeated for other legal professionals involved in the case? If the child has to testify, can she do so on video instead of in the courtroom? Ask your lawyer for advice on keeping your child out of the legal limelight.

- *Help older children constructively channel their feelings of anger or helplessness.* Activity can give children back their sense of control. Give your child some examples of what she can do, such as writing to her congresspeople about increasing aid for medical research on the disease affecting her or another family member, or doing some volunteer work for organizations that raise money for medical research or fight community violence.

• *If recovery is not expected, make preparations for last wishes.*
  Children who are old enough to understand that they are dying
  should be asked about anything they haven't had a chance to do
  or say and should be given every opportunity to accomplish these
  things. In fact, there are a number of organizations that you can
  call on to assist you. Ask your hospital social worker or your
  pediatrician. If an adult is not expected to recover, children should
  be informed so that they can make time to be with the relative
  and do any special activities that they might want to do while the
  adult is still lucid and functioning.

  When an adult has an illness or injury that might be fatal, it
  would be helpful to read Chapter 5, which explains children's
  perception of death and the stages of mourning. Mourning doesn't
  always start at the moment of death. Children might begin to
  mourn when they know that a relative is dying.

10

TRAUMA BY PROXY

Too Close for Comfort

This chapter is concerned with the traumatic effects of terrible *real* events that children hear about or are exposed to through the media or otherwise. When the actual catastrophic event happens to someone else, but the child—who could be miles away and who may not know the victim—develops posttraumatic symptoms almost as if the trauma happened to him or her, it's called trauma by proxy.

WHAT YOU SHOULD KNOW ABOUT TRAUMA BY PROXY

Children are more vulnerable than adults to being traumatized by distant events. Kids are particularly at risk of developing posttraumatic symptoms after being exposed to events in which they identify with the victim. Preschoolers who see pictures of dead or injured toddlers being carried away from the site of the Oklahoma City bombing, teens who learn about the suicide of Kurt Cobain on the radio, and young girls who watch graphic coverage on the evening news of the abduction of ten-year-old Polly Klaas from her home are vulnerable to developing posttraumatic reactions.

Kids can have intense emotional and behavioral reactions to traumatic events that happen *around* them but not *to* them, such as these:

• A schoolmate dies in a car accident or fire.

- A teenager in the child's school or town or even in a neighboring community commits suicide.
- A classmate develops cancer.
- A sibling or friend who has been through a traumatic experience "spreads" his or her posttraumatic symptoms by sharing graphic details of the event with peers, which leads to "contagion" of the posttraumatic reaction.
- A schoolmate is seriously injured in school violence.
- Random violence in the community confronts the child every day.
- A parent of a friend develops a fatal illness.
- A parent of a friend is injured or killed in a workplace accident.
- A parent of a friend is injured or killed in a car accident, plane crash, or commuter railroad accident.

YOUNG CHILDREN AND THE MEDIA

Kids of all ages are vulnerable to developing posttraumatic stress reactions when they are exposed to heavy media coverage of major disasters or violent crimes on television. However, preschool and school-age children in particular are frightened by these images. The world becomes a dangerous place, not just for the child who is actually caught by the stray bullet in Sarajevo, but also for the children in Dayton, Ohio, who only see pictures of the wounded child lying in the street. These children don't have the geographical safety zone that their parents have; they don't know that the war is happening halfway around the world and won't affect them.

Even children who are a little older can't always understand that the images broadcast into their living rooms reflect singular and often unusual events that are unlikely to be reenacted in their neighborhood. Through television, the Rodney King beating didn't happen on a street in Los Angeles, it happened in living rooms all across the country over and over again. Many young children who witnessed that violent event worried that such a thing could happen to them or to their father or older brother.

Television isn't the only news medium that brings images of violence to children. They also see horrific images on the cover of newsmagazines when the mail is delivered or on the front page of the newspaper left at the front door: a shot of Susan Smith's car being dredged from the lake or a photograph of a young girl crying in the president's arms during his visit to a relief center following the Midwest floods. Children are not inured to these images as adults are. They put themselves in the place of the children in those pictures and worry that these terrible things could happen to them.

This is not to suggest in any way that the media should be censored or controlled. The concern is that adults be aware that children can be traumatized by news reports and by images. Adults can then take the responsibility of talking to children about what they've seen or heard that has distressed them. The four-step method of debriefing can help with this task.

HOW CHILDREN REACT TO TRAUMA BY PROXY

Trauma by proxy is filtered through a child's perception of the world. Youngsters in varying age groups have different understandings of and reactions to catastrophic events that they hear about or see in the media. Let's take two examples—images of injured children in the Oklahoma City bombing and the news about a classmate killed in a car crash—and see how they are perceived at different ages.

Preschoolers (Ages Two to Five)

Children in this age group have a hard time distinguishing fantasy from reality, and their grasp of geography is limited. When they see a picture of a child who is hurt, they wonder if they might be at risk of being hurt in the same fashion. Although the children may be in New York, they don't understand that Oklahoma City is far away, nor do they understand the unusualness of the circumstances in which the child in the picture was hurt. They just worry that what happened to that little person might happen to them.

Trying to explain such complex issues as distance or terrorism or mental illness to a child of this age is impossible. Preschool children have enough trouble keeping the narrative of a story straight. They get the beginning, middle, and end of what they are told confused. Sometimes they forget one part and focus entirely on another. You may say that the child in the picture of the war lives very far away and that what happened there isn't likely to happen where your child lives, but the youngster might only remember that the child was hurt during a fight. If adults argue in the house, the little one might worry about getting hurt like the child in the picture because of the "fight."

On the other hand, hearing about a schoolmate who was killed in a car crash might not have as much of an impact on a preschooler who has never been in a car crash. Children in this age group don't understand the concept of death, nor can they imagine what a car crash is like. The story is too abstract to have much impact.

School-Age Children (Ages Six to Twelve)

School-age children have a much greater understanding of what they see and hear in the media, but their grasp on reality has a mixed effect. On the one hand, youngsters in this age group may be reassured by their understanding that the bombing in Oklahoma City happened in a distant place and that the likelihood of such an event in their neighborhood is slim. On the other hand, school-age children *do* understand what it means that a classmate was killed in a car crash, and they are aware that they, too, could be hurt while riding in a car. These children begin to realize that adults can't always provide protection from harm. This frightening revelation makes them feel vulnerable; consequently, they see the world in general as a riskier place in which to live.

When school-age youngsters hear about a trauma that strikes close to home or that affects a child in similar circumstances to their own even in a faraway place, they may find the situation so disturbing that they want to block it out of their minds. They don't want to talk about the incident or about anything that reminds them of what happened. They simply turn their thoughts away from anything related to the event. For instance, not only will a youngster not want to talk about what happened to his schoolmate who died in a car crash, but he also won't want to talk about the upcoming Little League season if the child in the accident was on his team.

Blocking out thoughts about the trauma or anything related to it has consequences for a child because she won't be able to stop the anxiety and fearfulness from spreading to situations farther and farther removed from the original trauma. Eventually, her inhibition of thoughts in any way related to the trauma will affect her relationships with her friends and her academic performance.

Though school-age children may not want to confront anxiety-provoking thoughts about a classmate who was killed, they will often focus on the death indirectly through play. You might see, for instance, your youngster playing a repetitive game of car crash and virtually ignoring the rest of his toys. However, even though it's obvious that he's preoccupied with his schoolmate's death, he still won't want to talk about it.

Teenagers (Ages Thirteen to Eighteen)

Teenagers have a mature grasp of the events they hear about and see. They understand not only the immediate event, but the underlying implications behind the event. Teens are not as likely as young children to be frightened by the images of injured children in Oklahoma City, not only because they understand that the event happened far away, but also because they can comprehend the sociopolitical issues that led to the bombing and how uncommon such a catastrophic event is.

However, adolescents will react more to traumas that happen to their peers than to catastrophes that occur in the world. Unlike younger children, peers are the most important group for teens. These kids neither confide in their parents nor value their opinions as they did when they were younger. They depend instead on their friends for their emotional grounding. Teens identify with *all* kids of their own age—even those who live far away and aren't a part of their group of friends.

Because teens are so directly affected by what happens to their counterparts, they often respond to trauma by proxy in a very personal manner. When they hear about a teenager getting killed in a car crash, they are struck by how little control they really have over their own life and death. This realization can interrupt their normal development. Teens who have started dating may stop and may even isolate themselves from their friends. What's the point of building relationships when you might die at any moment like the kid in the car crash? The same attitude can affect teenagers' interest in academic achievement, and consequently their performance in school can suffer. Teens sometimes react by indulging in risky behavior, such as smoking, drinking, or even driving hazardously, all because life suddenly seems far less certain than it did before the traumatic event occurred.

DEBRIEFING FOR TRAUMA BY PROXY

There is no practical way of protecting children from news reports or school rumors. Even if there were, completely censoring what youngsters see and hear is not in their best interest. Bearing witness to the atrocities happening in the world may awaken empathy and outrage at wrongdoing. In general, parents want their children to be sensitive to injustice and tragedy in the world but don't want them to be overwhelmed.

Simply saying that the trauma happened to someone else will not allay children's worries. To protect them, we have to give them the skills to handle and channel the feelings of fear, disgust, or anger that can be evoked by witnessing or hearing about horrifying events. When you debrief for trauma by proxy, keep these goals in mind.

You don't have to launch into a debriefing every time a disturbing image appears in the paper or on the television screen. Follow your child's lead. If she seems agitated or upset, fearful or moody, or if you notice a change in her academic or social standing following an incident in the community or a nationally broadcast calamity, that's the time to take steps to address the child's reactions to the trauma by proxy.

The following guidelines will help you make the debriefing more meaningful in situations of trauma by proxy. The four-step debriefing method is discussed in general terms in Chapter 4.

Step I: Preparing Yourself

- *Reread Chapters 3 and 4.*   You'll want to familiarize yourself with the reactions that children of different ages have to events that traumatize them and to review the four steps of debriefing.
- *Find out the details of the situation.*   If you don't already know about the event that traumatized your child, now is the time to do your detective work and get the whole story from sources other than your child before talking with him or her.

Step II: Having the Child Tell the Story

- *Start the debriefing by making a comment or observation about the traumatic event.* Returning to the example of the Oklahoma City bombing, you might start the debriefing by saying, "The news from Oklahoma City is pretty scary. What do you think the kids who have gone to look at the building are thinking and worrying about?" This will provide an opening for the child to talk about what he knows about the traumatic event.

Step III: Sharing the Child's Reaction

- *Talk about reactions that you've noticed.* You might say to your child, "I noticed in the assembly for the boy who committed suicide that you were upset. It is very sad when someone takes his own life."
- *Talk about what you are feeling and thinking.* In the case of a suicide, you might say, "When someone your age kills himself, teens sometimes feel that the adults are to blame because they either didn't notice what was wrong or didn't do anything. It's sad, too, because sometimes adults can't stop terrible things from happening. But we do try. We try very hard. You should know that. You should also know that the sad, angry feelings go away. It just takes time."

Step IV: Survival and Recovery

In this step, the strategies you use will depend on the age of your child.

Preschoolers (Ages Two to Five)
- *Turn off the television news.* If your young child balks at seeing violence on the news, try to cooperate with her by turning off the evening news and making a habit of watching the late-night news instead. Say, "I can see that was upsetting to you. I know that was a scary picture, and I'll be more careful about what you see on television so you won't be frightened again."
- *Reassure your child that the traumatic event is unlikely to happen to him.* Explain that what the child saw, whether it was a

war-torn city or a place ravaged by natural disaster, happened in a faraway place and that such terrible things do not happen very often. Let the child know that even if there were a terrible storm or fire, you would do everything possible to make sure that he was kept safe.

School-Age Children (Ages Six to Twelve)

School-age children understand more of what they see and hear on the news and in the community, and they need more concrete information about how they would be protected in the event of a disaster. Obviously, what you say to reassure your child depends on what she saw. Here are some examples:

- *If your child saw a terrible fire, show her the smoke and carbon-monoxide detectors in the home.* Let her help you change the batteries regularly. You also can tell her how she would escape in the event of a fire, via a fire escape or window ladders.
- *If your child saw a natural disaster, explain why the disaster wouldn't happen where you live.* If you live in an area where severe storms and earthquakes do occur, detail the steps you would take to protect the family.
- *If your child heard about an abduction, show her how to lock her windows and how the rest of the house is secured against intruders.* This is also a good time to make sure that she knows her address and phone number as well as how to use 911 to get help in an emergency.

Teenagers (Ages Thirteen to Eighteen)

Teenagers have a fairly mature perspective on what they see, but they often feel at a loss in terms of what they can do about terrible situations they hear about. Again, you have to tailor your advice to the specific event in question, but here are some examples:

- *In the case of school violence, help your child participate in or develop a conflict resolution program in school.* These programs give students a place to go with their grievances before a fight erupts.
- *In the case of teen suicide, make your child aware of community suicide hotlines where kids with emotional problems can get help.*

You can also help a teen understand that when a friend says that he or she is feeling suicidal, the child's loyalty is best shown not by keeping a secret, but by alerting an adult so that the friend can get the help that is needed.

• *In the case of a natural disaster or war, you can make your teen aware of relief efforts.* Explain how he can contribute by starting a food drive or some other community effort to help disaster victims.

The aim of debriefing for trauma by proxy is to help the child feel less impotent. You want to give the child information and options to help him feel that he can take some action either to protect himself or to help others.

PART THREE

APPENDIXES

APPENDIX 1
FINDING A THERAPIST

Choosing a therapist can be a bewildering process. There are not only different kids of therapies, but also different types of therapists: clinical social workers, marriage and family counselors, psychologists, and psychiatrists. In most states, anyone can hang out a shingle advertising "psychotherapy," but only these few professional categories are recognized by most state licensing boards. A professional who is licensed will have proof available, usually a certificate on the wall or on the desk. Licensed professionals should also carry professional malpractice insurance. Although it is unlikely that you will have a complaint against a therapist, it is in your interest to make sure that the therapist you choose is licensed and insured—just as you would expect your family physician to be.

Clinical social workers have completed a two-year post-baccalaureate program with a specialization in understanding people within their social context. Marriage and family counselors have completed a two-year postcollege degree program specializing in marriage and family issues.

Psychologists have doctorates usually earned after four to six years of postbaccalaureate study. They specialize in the study of human behavior and are trained in the administration and application of psychological tests.

Psychiatrists are medical doctors who have taken specialized training (a residency) in illnesses of the mind. A psychiatrist will hold a license to practice medicine and should be board-certified in psychiatry. Psychiatrists are the only therapists who can prescribe medications, such as antidepressants.

Most therapists suggest that the prospective patient get a few names from friends, family members, pediatricians, school guidance counselors, and company-sponsored employee assistance programs and then shop around. Don't hesitate to ask the therapist questions: What training and experience have you had in working with children? What training and experience have you had in trauma? How do you work with children? Do you include parent counseling? How long will the therapy take? How much will it cost?

APPENDIX 2
WHAT TO EXPECT FROM THERAPY

In general, psychotherapy today tends to fall into two broad categories. One is a highly focused treatment that tackles a specific set of symptoms by directly modifying thinking and behavior. The second is a more global approach that seeks to effect a major personality change.

Trauma work, for the most part, falls within the first approach. It is results oriented and usually moves quickly. However, if a child has been horribly traumatized or traumatized repeatedly over a long period of time, the psychotherapy will likely take longer. First, the child will need time to develop trust in the therapist. Then it will take time to unravel the many ways the ongoing trauma shaped the child's development and psyche.

Young children often do not have the words to describe events that were frightening or confusing, and thus they communicate their concern to the therapist through play. Play is children's way of telling the therapist what happened and how they feel about it. Older children will communicate with the therapist verbally, but even teens might have an easier time telling their story through role play, puppets, games, or drawing pictures.

If your child is seeing a therapist, you should expect to meet with the therapist, too. The therapist will not be treating you but will likely want to know how your child is doing outside the sessions. (After all, it's not the child's behavior in session that counts, but how the child is doing emotionally in school and at home.) The therapist will also likely offer you tips, ideas, and techniques that you can use to help in your child's recovery.

FURTHER READING*

Children and Trauma

Adults

Post-Traumatic Stress Disorder in Children, edited by Spencer Eth and Robert Pynoos (Washington, D.C.: American Psychiatric Press, 1984)

Debriefing

Adults

"Individual and Small Group Psychotherapy for Children Involved in Trauma and Disaster," by H. Gillis, in *Children and Disasters,* edited by C. Saylor (New York: Plenum Press, 1993)

Death

Adults

The Season of Grief: Helping Children Grow through Loss, by Donna A. Gaffnex (New York: Penguin, 1988)

To Read with Children

How It Feels When a Parent Dies, by Jill Krementz (New York: Alfred A. Knopf, 1993)

---

*For all books recommended here as "to read with children," be sure to first read the book yourself to see if you agree with the particular presentation.

Abuse

Adults
Spiders and Flies: Help for Parents and Teachers of Sexually Abused Children, by D. Hillman and J. Solek-Tefft (New York: Macmillan, 1988)

To Read with Children
My Body Is Private, by L. Girard (Morton Grove, Ill.: Albert Whitman, 1984)
Hear My Roar: A Story of Family Violence, by T. Hochban and B. Krykorka (Toronto: Annick Press, 1994)

Natural Disasters

Adults
Impact of Natural Disasters on Children and Families, by R. W. Belter and P. S. Mitsuko, in *Children and Disasters,* edited by C. Saylor (New York: Plenum Press, 1993)

To Read with Children
A Coloring Book: After the Tornado, by B. F. Corder and T. Haizlip (printed by the North Carolina Division of Mental Health, Mental Retardation, and Substance Abuse under grant #1 HO7MH000016-01 from The National Institute of Mental Health.) Available through the Red Cross. In addition, the Red Cross offers other books on a variety of natural disasters.

Divorce

Adults
Growing up with Divorce: Helping Your Child Avoid Immediate and Later Emotional Problems, by N. Kalter (New York: Fawcett/Columbine, 1990)

To Read with Children
Dinosaurs Divorce: A Guide for Changing Families, by L. K. Brown and M. Brown (Boston: Little, Brown, 1986)

Illness and Injury

Adults
"Post-Traumatic Stress Disorder in Children with Cancer," by Y. Nir, in *Post-Traumatic Stress Disorder in Children,* edited by Spencer Eth and Robert Pynoos (Washington, D.C.: American Psychiatric Press, 1984)

To Read with Children
Why Am I Going to the Hospital, by C. Ciliotta and C. Livingston (New York: Carol, 1992)
When Mommy Is Sick, by F. Sherkin-Langer (Morton Grove, Ill.: Albert Whitman, 1995)

Trauma by Proxy

To Read with Children
Why Did It Happen? Helping Children Cope in a Violent World, by J. Cohn (New York: Morrow Junior Books, 1994)

INDEX

ABOUT THE AUTHORS

Barbara Brooks was born in Brooklyn, New York, and grew up in Miami Beach, Florida. She received her bachelor of arts degree from Brooklyn College and her doctor of philosophy degree in clinical psychology from the University of Massachusetts in Amherst. She completed her internship and fellowship in child psychology at The New York Hospital–Cornell Medical Center.

Dr. Brooks was a staff psychologist for teenagers at Hawthorn Cedar Knolls School, a residential treatment center in Hawthorn, New York. She is currently Clinical Director of CH/ECP, Inc. The firm specializes in responding to psychiatric needs after a disaster or emergency. In addition, CH/ECP provides general employee assistance programs and counseling. Dr. Brooks has responded on site to disasters such as Hurricane Andrew, the World Trade Center bombing, and the Northridge earthquake. Dr. Brooks has been an educator, serving as lecturer for the University of Maryland in Germany, where she presented seminars on trauma and abuse to members of the U.S. military, and as adjunct instructor at Yeshiva University Graduate School of Social Work.

Dr. Brooks has written frequently for professional journals. She has also been quoted in popular books and in magazines. She has appeared on the news magazine show *Inside Edition*, ABC TV News, CNBC TV, an educational cable station in New York, and NBC radio.

Dr. Brooks maintains a private practice in New York and is a principal in Trauma Recovery Associates, a center for the counseling of trauma victims and their families and the training of mental health professionals in the counseling of trauma victims.

Paula M. Siegel grew up in Albany, New York, and received her bachelor of arts degree in journalism at Syracuse University. Currently, she lives in Manhattan with her two sons, Will and George.

Ms. Siegel has written about health and psychology for more than two decades. Her articles on parenting, relationships, and health have appeared regularly in such national publications as *Mademoiselle, Good Housekeeping, Redbook, Self, Glamour, Working Mother*, and *GQ*. She is also the author of seven other books.

Ms. Siegel is a member of the Author's Guild and the American Society of Journalists and Authors.